WALKI

WEST

C000108941

Paul Hannon

HILLSIDE

HILLSIDE GUIDES - ACROSS THE NORTH

Long Distance Walks
- •COAST TO COAST WALK
- •CLEVELAND WAY COMPANION
- •WESTMORLAND WAY
- •FURNESS WAY
- •CUMBERLAND WAY
- •DALES WAY
- •LADY ANNE'S WAY
- •NORTH BOWLAND TRAVERSE

Circular Walks - Lancashire
- •BOWLAND
- •PENDLE & THE RIBBLE

Circular Walks - Yorkshire Dales
- •HOWGILL FELLS
- •THREE PEAKS
- •MALHAMDALE
- •WHARFEDALE
- •NIDDERDALE
- •WENSLEYDALE
- •SWALEDALE

Circular Walks - North York Moors
- •WESTERN MOORS
- •SOUTHERN MOORS
- •NORTHERN MOORS

Circular Walks - South Pennines
- •BRONTE COUNTRY
- •CALDERDALE
- •ILKLEY MOOR

Circular Walks - Peak District
- •EASTERN PEAK
- •NORTHERN PEAK
- •CENTRAL PEAK
- •SOUTHERN PEAK
- •WESTERN PEAK

Circular Walks - North Pennines
- •TEESDALE
- •EDEN VALLEY

Hillwalking - Lake District
- •OVER LAKELAND MOUNTAINS
- •OVER LAKELAND FELLS

Yorkshire Pub Walks
- •HARROGATE/WHARFE VALLEY
- •HAWORTH/AIRE VALLEY

Large format colour hardback

FREEDOM OF THE DALES

BIKING COUNTRY
- •YORKSHIRE DALES CYCLE WAY
- •WEST YORKSHIRE CYCLE WAY
- •MOUNTAIN BIKING - WEST & SOUTH YORKSHIRE
- •AIRE VALLEY BIKING GUIDE
- •CALDERDALE BIKING GUIDE
- • GLASGOW Clyde Valley & Loch Lomond

• YORK WALKS *City Theme Walks*

•WALKING COUNTRY TRIVIA QUIZ *Over 1000 questions*

Send S.A.E. for up-to-date details and pricelist

WALKING COUNTRY

WESTERN PEAK

Paul Hannon

HILLSIDE

HILLSIDE
PUBLICATIONS
11 Nessfield Grove
Keighley
West Yorkshire
BD22 6NU

First published 1997

© Paul Hannon 1997

ISBN 1 870141 54 7

The author would like to acknowledge the assistance of Roland Smith, Head of Information Services at the Peak National Park, for his invaluable help in looking over the manuscript. Any errors, however, remain the author's.

Cover illustrations:
Grin Low, Buxton; above Wettonmill; Lyme Park
Back cover: Warslow Brook
(Paul Hannon/Big Country Picture Library)

Page 1: The Bow Stones, Lyme Park
Page 3: Eagle & Child, near Gradbach

Printed in Great Britain by
Carnmor Print and Design
95-97 London Road
Preston
Lancashire
PR1 4BA

CONTENTS

*PLEASE NOTE:
Above mileages incorrect for
the following walks, correct
mileages in brackets:
11(7¼) 12(7) 14(6) 15(7¾)
16(8¼) 17(8¾) 18(6½) 19(7½)
(all are correct in their
relevant chapter)*

INTRODUCTION

THE PEAK NATIONAL PARK

The Peak District was designated Britain's first National Park in 1951, and embracing an area of 555 square miles it is the most popular in the country. While commonly allotted to Derbyshire, substantial parts fall within Staffordshire, Yorkshire and Cheshire. *Peak* is in fact a misnomer, for it is plainly evident that peaks are in very short supply here: it derives from *Pecsaetan* ('hill-dweller'), tribes that occupied the area long before the Normans came.

The Peak divides into two distinctive areas, the Dark Peak and the White Peak. These refer to the principal rocks, millstone grit (gritstone) in the Dark Peak and limestone in the White Peak. The Dark Peak horseshoe encloses the limestone country, with the high moors of Kinder Scout and Bleaklow to the north and long arms reaching down either side. That in the east traces the Derwent Valley south in a series of abrupt edges: that to the west is disjointed, resurrecting itself above Buxton to run south, largely less dramatically, west of the Manifold Valley. The northern massif is typified by vast tracts of peat bog and heather, a world away from the White Peak's softer terrain.

The compact White Peak offers green dales overlooked by gleaming cliffs. Unlike the limestone country of the Yorkshire Dales, it has few potholes and pavements: its speciality is valleys, exemplified by the likes of Lathkill Dale, the river Wye and the incomparable Dovedale. Much of the White Peak is an upland plateau where old lead mining communities huddle. The area is dissected by drystone walls, and though large-scale quarrying is all too evident, farming remains the traditional source of employment, increasingly supplemented by tourism. While one railway survives to run through the heart of the Park, several others have been converted to leisure trails: they provide excellent cross-country routes linking numerous towns and villages.

Bakewell is the largest community in the National Park, but it is the small towns on the fringe, such as Buxton, Ashbourne, Matlock, Leek, Chapel en le Frith and Glossop, that act as major centres. Though this whole area might be encircled in a day's car tour, once you get out in the fresh air you will quickly appreciate the rich diversity of country that offers many happy years of real exploring - on foot.

WESTERN PEAK

The Western Peak embraces outstandingly varied walking country from the splendour of Lyme Park to the heathery, gritstone scarps of the Roaches, and stretches from the windswept moors of Axe Edge and Morridge to the limestone secrets of the Manifold Valley. Most of the area falls within Staffordshire, while Cheshire also ensures that Derbyshire sees little of the Western Peak.

Though perhaps the least frequented area of the Peak District, certain parts are extremely well known. Popular visitor haunts include Tegg's Nose, Grin Low and Macclesfield Forest, while the Goyt Valley has long been a major attraction. The Roaches and the Manifold Valley are probably most visited, and walkers and tourists alike can easily link the latter with its more celebrated neighbour Dovedale, in the Southern Peak. Limestone features such as Thor's Cave, Beeston Tor and the Sugarloaf dominate an area where the shy rivers Manifold and Hamps seek subterranean courses. Just a few miles to the west these White Peak highlights are countered by such gritstone delights as Ramshaw Rocks, Lud's Church and the incomparable Roaches.

The lesser known Dane Valley is a real ace in the pack, featuring truly beautiful, often richly wooded countryside around Wincle, Back Forest and Three Shires Head. Highest inhabited part of the Peak, the Staffordshire Moorlands secrete the village of Flash, claiming to be the highest in England. Villages are scarce in this wilder gritstone country: more typical are scattered settlements such as Wildboarclough, Gradbach and Danebridge. Onecote, Waterfall, Upper Hulme and Meerbrook are small, unassuming communities, while the Manifold Valley offers more traditional villages such as Wetton, Grindon, Warslow and Butterton.

In marked contract to this sparsely populated region is the bustling town of Buxton. Though well placed for most of the Peak, its true allegiance is to this western area, where steep-flanked hills rise above deep valleys. Undemanding ascents are made to the super viewpoints of Shutlingsloe, Gun, Hen Cloud and Shining Tor. Historical interest includes caves occupied by Man 10,000 years ago; monastic granges; a labyrinthian network of packhorse trails; and abandoned railways in the Goyt and Manifold Valleys.

This then is the Western Peak: heather moors, limestone tors, sweeping views and plenty of room to move.

Access

Unlike the northern moors and eastern edges, which cover vast tracts of rolling moorland and are subject to numerous access agreements, the remainder of the Peak can be accessed largely without problem using the extensive rights of way network. The various moors of the Western Peak are reasonably well served by paths, so that the only times we resort to non rights of way are on occasions where concession paths have been negotiated or offered to open up popular areas. Examples in this book are around the Goyt Valley, the Roaches and Back Forest, the latter being within land owned by the National Park. The Authority also has small but important access areas at Ramshaw Rocks and Merryton Low. Additionally, sections of the Manifold Track are used in similar fashion.

Please take extra care to respect the life and work of the Peak. Its very accessibility puts it in the firing line when we all want to escape to the countryside at the same time. If we take nothing more than photographs and leave only the slightest of footprints, this wonderful landscape will be in good shape for the next generation. In particular, ensure that dogs are kept on leads and that you close any gates that you have opened.

*The Roaches
from Hen Cloud*

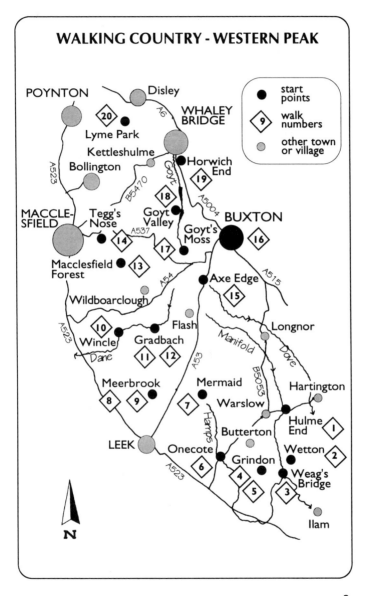

WALKING COUNTRY - WESTERN PEAK

Legend:
- ● start points
- ◆9 walk numbers
- ● other town or village

POYNTON

Disley

Lyme Park

WHALEY BRIDGE

◆20

Kettleshulme

Horwich End

Bollington

◆19

◆18

MACCLESFIELD

Tegg's Nose

Goyt Valley

Goyt's Moss

BUXTON

◆16

◆14

◆17

Macclesfield Forest

◆13

Axe Edge

◆15

Wildboarclough

Flash

Longnor

◆10

Wincle

Gradbach

◆11 ◆12

Dane

Meerbrook

Mermaid

Hartington

◆8 ◆9

Warslow

Hulme End

◆7

Butterton

◆1

LEEK

Onecote

Grindon

Wetton

◆6

◆4

◆2

◆5

Weag's Bridge

◆3

Ilam

N

9

Getting around

Buxton is the focal point of the area, being well placed for access to virtually all these walks, and served by bus and train from the outside world. Other well sited towns include Leek, Macclesfield and Whaley Bridge, with all but Leek having rail stations. The A53 Buxton-Leek road is strategic for accessing many walks, both by car and by bus. Limited bus services radiate to many of the villages.

Numerous seasonal bus services also operate on less regular routes. With a little planning, various permutations can be created by linking different sections of the walks, to create longer routes or to take advantage of public transport. Starting points with public transport, however limited, are indicated, along with other useful information, at the start of each walk.

Using the guide

Each walk is self-contained, with essential information being followed by a simple map and concise description of the route. Dovetailed between this are useful notes of features along the way, and interspersed are illustrations which both capture the flavour of the walks and record the many items of interest. In order to make the instructions easier to follow, essential route description has been highlighted in bold type, while items in lighter type refer to historical asides and things to look out for: in this format you can find your way more easily while still locating features of interest at the relevant point in the text.

The simple sketch maps identify the location of the routes rather than the fine detail, and whilst the route description should be sufficient to guide you around, an Ordnance Survey map is recommended: the route can easily be plotted on the relevant OS map. To gain the most from a walk, the detail of the 1:25,000 maps is unsurpassed. They also serve to vary walks as desired, giving an improved picture of one's surroundings and the availability of linking paths. Just one map covers all but one of the walks:-

• *Outdoor Leisure Sheet 24 - Peak District, White Peak*

Walk 20 is the odd one out, being found on the companion map:-

• *Outdoor Leisure Sheet 1 - Peak District, Dark Peak*

Also extremely useful for general planning purposes are the Landranger maps at 1:50,000, and three sheets cover the area:

109, Manchester;   118, Stoke-on-Trent & Macclesfield
119, Buxton, Matlock & Dove Dale

One further planning aid is the OS Touring Map which covers the entire National Park at the scale of 1:63,360 (1 inch to the mile).

SOME USEFUL ADDRESSES

Ramblers' Association 1/5 Wandsworth Road, London SW8 2XX
Tel. 0171-339 8500

Peak National Park Office
Aldern House, Baslow Road, Bakewell DE45 1AE   Tel. 01629-816200

Tourist Information
The Crecent **Buxton** Derbyshire SK17 6BQ
Tel. 01298-25106
Market Place **Leek** Staffordshire ST13 5HH
Tel. 01538-381000
Town Hall, Market Place **Macclesfield** Cheshire SK10 1DX
Tel. 01625-504114

Peak & Northern Footpaths Society
Mr E Sutton, 1 Crossfield Grove, Marple Bridge, Cheshire SK6 5EQ
Tel. 0161-427 3582

Friends of National Parks
Council for National Parks, 246 Lavender Hill, London SW11 1LJ
Tel. 071-924 4077

Staffordshire Wildlife Trust
Coutts House, Sandon, Stafford ST18 0DN
Tel. 01889-508534

Cheshire Wildlife Trust
Grebe House, Reaseheath, Nantwich, Cheshire CW5 6DG
Tel. 01270-610180

The National Trust
South Peak Estate Office Home Farm, Ilam, nr. Ashbourne,
Derbyshire DE6 2AZ   Tel. 01335-350503
Lyme Park Disley, Stockport SK12 2NX   Tel. 01663-762023

British Rail, Buxton line
Tel. 0161-234 3157 (Manchester)

Busline, Buxton Tel. 01298-23098

ECTON & BUTTERTON

START *Hulme End*   *Grid ref. SK 102593*

DISTANCE *8½ miles*

ORDNANCE SURVEY MAPS
1:50,000
Landranger 119 - Buxton, Matlock & Dove Dale
1:25,000
Outdoor Leisure 24 - Peak District, White Peak

ACCESS Start from the large car park at the head of the Manifold Track on the B5054, west of Hartington. Served by Hartington-Buxton buses and other less frequent services, including Postbus from Leek.

Lots of ups and downs in a lively exploration of the Manifold Valley.

S   Hulme End was the northern terminus of the Leek & Manifold Light Railway, and its restored booking office is now the Manifold Valley Visitor Centre, with toilets. The old engine sheds are also still in place. Hulme End's pub just across the river is the pleasant *Manifold Valley Hotel*, previously the *Light Railway Hotel*, while there is also a useful shop in the hamlet.

The ill-starred railway opened in 1904 as a single track line. Of its ten stations, all but the termini were tiny halts at such places as Thor's Cave, their valley locations intended to serve villages on the plateau. Its eight miles from Waterhouses to Hulme End had little success: anticipated trade from copper mines re-opening at Ecton never materialised, and closure of the creamery at Ecton was the final straw. The last train ran on March 2nd, 1934. Very enterprisingly for the time, the county council stepped in and surfaced the route for leisure use. Now known as the Manifold Track, its hard surface makes longer excursions more suited to cycling than walking.

Start off along the tarmac surface of the Manifold Track. At once it forges into steeper flanked country as the Manifold Valley takes real shape. After a short mile the way arrives at Dale Bridge, Ecton. The easy option forges straight on the track, remaining on it to Wettonmill, an immensely attractive couple of miles (see WALK 3). The main route, however, gets you off the track and onto the hills.

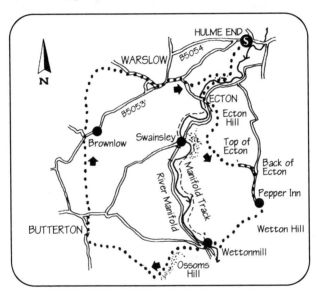

Turn left on the road up to a junction, right a few yards then up the private road on the left. It climbs steeply past a couple of houses to end at the Hillocks, a curious house also known as Radcliffe's Folly. This rustic folly was built in 1933 by the then MP for Leek, and now serves as a centre for mine exploration and study. The copper spire came from an old chapel, and makes a bizarre local landmark.

Pass along the front of the house, under an arch and up to a stile on the left. This gains the bottom corner of Ecton Hill. A good path heads along to the right, soon revealing its true purpose as it swings up the concave slope to make easy work of the climb as a well engineered green way. Ecton Hill was extensively worked for copper (unusual in a district where lead was the main objective), and old shafts and hollows abound. Mining took place over many years, the two main centuries of effort culminating in a late 18th century boom, when the Duke of Devonshire took staggering amounts that helped pay for his grand schemes in Buxton (e.g. building the Crescent).

Reaching a knoll at the end, the path becomes a thinner trod running high above the dale. Sweeping views down the valley include the big house at Swainsley, below. **The path runs falteringly on to a line of trees: angle left a few yards to a stile in the sturdy wall above. Now head directly away to a crumbling wall corner, then on to an intact one before branching right to a gateway at the end of the trees ahead.** The environs of Top of Ecton are outspread, with Summerhill Farm to the right and Broad Ecton Farm below. **Slant down to the far corner of the field, crossing a drive. From the stile go left with the wall to a stile onto the access road alongside a dewpond.**

Turn right on the road, over a brow and down to a junction. Go right, the road working past several houses to end at a lone house. This appealing three-storey building known as Pepper Inn (it once helped quench miners' thirsts) is over 250 years old and has seen various other uses including a spell as a factory. **Go straight on down to a stile and gate, and head downstream with a tiny trickle. Running between the Wetton Hills, this deep divide leads pleasantly away, the stream quickly disappearing underground. When the valley swings markedly left, a broad path is seen slanting up into the trees on the right.**

The path crosses a slender neck of land dividing our side valley from the Manifold, which appears in all its glory as we double back down the other side to Wettonmill. Just above the mill, look downstream for an impressive glimpse of Thor's Cave (see WALK 4). Our path emerges into the yard at the popular National Trust cafe, alongside the scenic riverside and bridge (illustrated on page 25).

Cross the bridge onto the road and straight over on the Butterton road. Almost at once this is left by a gate to its left (not the footbridge over the sidestream). A broad path heads away through the fields, forging on the floor of the increasingly attractive side valley of Hoo Brook. Open country leads along to a junction of ways at a tiny footbridge in a shady dell. Take the stile on the right and head across the field, the sharp turn of Hoo Brook keeping faith as a grand walk ensues. It points unerringly at Butterton (not seen until almost upon it), through numerous streamside pastures and crossing to the other side part way up.

Eventually a tiny waterfall is passed as the village is reached. Cross the stream onto a rough track. Either go left to the road and ford, or straight up the walled path to the road. The path emerges alongside the former school, now a tearoom offering us further refreshment.

St. Bartholomew's, Butterton

Butterton is a hilly but welcoming village, and the church spire beckons us to the top. St. Bartholomew's dates from 1873, its cosy interior smaller than the exterior suggests. A nice touch is a memorial to the Rev R J Crump, vicar for 39 years to 1953, alongside a photo of the village lads who went to war in 1914-1918 - also featuring Crump himself. Opposite the church the *Black Lion* pub sports a 1782 datestone, while a Post office/shop stands further along the road west.

Continue straight up the road to a junction past the church. Go right a few yards then head away on a rough lane. Emerging into fields, advance to a stile. A far-reaching panorama features our next village, Warslow; the moorland of Revidge behind; and old friend Ecton Hill to the right. **More colourful country is entered as the route forges straight on, descending a steeper slope to the wide defile of Warslow Brook. A sturdy footbridge will be found to cross it. Rise past a lone gatepost, up the hedge-side to the B5053.**

Go right to the Elkstone road, along it a few yards and over a stile on the right. Head up two field-sides to a barn, continuing up by a fence with a side valley forming on the left. Simply advance straight up, a path forming and gradually becoming enclosed. An improving green track rises all the way, a grand climb. Retrospective views feature two spires and an archetypal landscape of fields, trees and hedgerows. **At the top the track turns right and runs on to absorb the drive at Water Gap Farm before emerging onto the road at the top of Warslow.**

Spread unassumingly down a hillside, Warslow was originally an estate village of the Harpur Crewe family. St. Lawrence's church of 1820 stands in the centre. Village pub is the *Greyhound*, while there are also a Primitive Methodist Chapel of 1848, a tiny Post office, village hall, modern school drawing from the local villages, and a shop on the B5053 going out. The old school is now an activity centre.

Descend through the village to a junction with the B5053 again. Turn left along the road, then right at the first junction. Keep right at the next junction, descending to a corner and take a stile in front. Head away with the wall contouring round the slope. The Manifold Valley of the walk's early stages is now outspread, a fine sight - particularly Ecton Hill and Radcliffe's Folly. **A wall drops back down from the left and is followed along above a hawthorn bank, a faint path running on for some time before dropping down at the end to join the Manifold Track. Go left for five minutes to finish.**

2

HIDDEN MANIFOLD

START Wetton   Grid ref. SK 109553

DISTANCE 9 miles

ORDNANCE SURVEY MAPS
1:50,000
Landranger 119 - Buxton, Matlock & Dove Dale
1:25,000
Outdoor Leisure 24 - Peak District, White Peak

ACCESS Start from the pub and tiny green in the village centre. There is a car park/toilets at the southern end. Served by market day buses from Ashbourne and by Postbus from Leek.

S Wetton is a hugely attractive village centred around a tiny green on a road junction. Across it stands the welcoming *Royal Oak* pub. St. Margaret's church stands just above: rebuilt in 1820, the tower has survived from the 14th century. There is also a chapel of 1870 and farm refreshments just down from the green.

Leave the green by descending the road to the next junction. Note a most impressive barn on the right here. **The branch right goes to the car park, but we exit the village only a few yards along it at a stile set back on the left. Cross a small field and caravan site drive to another stile then head diagonally away. Beyond an acute field corner continue rising to a barn on the brow. Just short of it, take a stile near the wall corner on the left.** The Manifold Valley makes its first appearance down to the right. **Descend the field-side onto a narrow, part-grassy back road (Larkstone Lane).**

Cross straight over and on to a stile just beyond, from where a path contours away to an opposite wall corner with a facing stile. Beneath, the head of a dry side valley forms rapidly, with fast increasing views. **The path slants up to the wall above and maintains this course for some time across the open bank. Beyond a crumbling wall it cuts across again to a sturdier wall above, and resumes along the steep bank of Bincliff.** The slope below is decorated by occasional hawthorn, nothing like the woodland suggested on the map. Far below, the Manifold Valley sweeps around its mighty course, the only thing usually missing being the river. Except in times of spate, it sinks below ground near Wettonmill and only re-appears at Ilam.

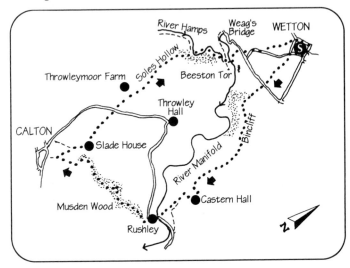

After a good half-mile, a small re-entrant is reached just after a stile. Here the way slants up to a stile on the left. The section of valley ahead is the Castern Wood nature reserve of Staffordshire Wildlife Trust. This varied habitat of deciduous woodland and steep limestone grassland has yielded over 240 species of plants and 40 species of breeding birds. The area was also an extensive 19th century lead mining site, old spoil heaps and adits (horizontal shafts) being the most plentiful evidence. A circular trail descends to the riverbank: there is no through route.

From the stile advance to a track in front of spoil heaps then turn right along it into a field. Slant down to the far corner where stile and gate await. This is point 289m on the map which, incidentally, depicts more field boundaries than actually survive. **Bear left towards the wall, but without joining it curve across the big concave field to find a stile/gate in the far corner.** Here are grand views updale to the great cliff of Beeston Tor, of which more later.

From the gate a grassy track heads away. Ignore the one branching up to the left, and keep straight on. Across the valley on our contour is an isolated farm, Throwley Hall. The remains of the 16th century house are in front of a 19th century replacement. **The track becomes firmer before arriving at an access road behind Castern Hall. Turn right along the road, round the side of the house.** This is a splendid three-storey residence dating from the 18th century, with a riot of springtime daffodils in the garden.

Castern Hall

The drive zigzags down the hill, though it can be short-cut by following the left-hand wall down. As the drive levels out the path drops down to join it, but goes only a few yards along before slanting down the vast pasture. A gap-stile awaits across the field, then crossing a line of trees to Rushley Bridge on the Manifold. Its dry vegetated bed is a curiously unnatural sight.

Cross the bridge and head along to Rushley Farm, leaving the road and continuing straight on between the buildings. At the bend beyond, leave the track before the cattle-grid on the near-side of the wall on the right. Squeezing past some pens including a pig pen, the way runs on to enter Musden Wood. A green path heads away up the floor of this dry valley, and a smashing walk ensues. The way leads up its winding floor between deep sided and wooded flanks: towards the top a primrose bank opens up on the right. **As the head is reached the path continues in a shady hollow through several pastures.**

With Calton village in sight ahead, our route doubles back on itself where a track goes up the wall-side on the right, just a couple of fields short of the road. At the wall corner above, it slants back up the wall/ hedge side then rises to join a grassy cart track. Over to the right beyond our erstwhile hollow, note the distinctive flat-topped Thorpe Cloud guarding the entrance to Dovedale. **Go right along the track to Slade House, then left on its drive which rises away through the fields. On the brow it passes dewponds then runs down to an open road.**

Go straight over and down a gradually forming hollow, passing a walled dewpond with another to come. At a wall corner the wall shadows us down. When a stile takes us to the other side an old green way runs down Soles Hollow, but at the true head of the little valley it turns off, leaving us to descend to a stile. Entering Old Soles Wood, a stony path descends through scrub woodland before opening out. At the bottom it plants us on the Manifold Track in the Hamps Valley. It will quickly be gleaned that the Hamps is normally as parched as the Manifold, only surfacing after copious spells of rain.

This surfaced way, a refuge for walkers, bikers and equestrians, is on the course of the former Leek & Manifold Light Railway from Waterhouses to Hulme End. Of the eight miles half is in the Hamps Valley, which merges with the Manifold under Beeston Tor, just ahead. For more on the line please refer to page 12. **Turn right along the track, crossing the dry river several times with Beeston Tor quickly appearing.** Here the Hamps undergoes its final yards before the non-event of its confluence with the parent river.

When bridle-gates appear on each side, that on the right leads past caravans to Beeston Tor farm drive. Go right towards the farm (passing the non-confluence), but then take a gate on the left to stepping stones on the Manifold. They are likely to be superfluous, but should the river be in spate, turn upstream to cross at Weag's Bridge. **The spectacular limestone buttress of Beeston Tor now towers impressively above.** In St. Bertram's Cave at its foot a hoard of Anglo-Saxon silver coins was discovered, but animal bones have yielded evidence of occupation by Man thousands of years earlier.

20

From the stile opposite cross to the base of the scrub bank, where a broad path slants up the bank away from the tor. Emerging into a field at the top, rise up the wall-side to join a narrow road (Larkstone Lane, again). Go right a few yards then take a stile above, climbing the centre of a punishingly steep field to a gap-stile onto another road, Carr Lane. Rise a little further, and as it levels out take a stile on the left.

Bear away from the road to a stile. Wetton's church tower is the first indication of the village appearing ahead. **Head on through a second stile then across to the field corner. An unsightly farm field is the last of the day, going forward to a concrete track leading down to the left of modern farm buildings. In the very corner a step-stile admits to a garden, crossing the edge of the lawn to another stile onto the road. Go right for the village centre.**

Beeston Tor from the dry Manifold

3

MANIFOLD VALLEY

START *Weag's Bridge*   *Grid ref. SK 099541*

DISTANCE *6¼ miles*

ORDNANCE SURVEY MAPS
1:50,000
Landranger 119 - Buxton, Matlock & Dove Dale
1:25,000
Outdoor Leisure 24 - Peak District, White Peak

ACCESS *Start from Weag's Bridge where the Grindon-Wetton road crosses the Manifold Valley: there is a good sized car park. Alternative starts are Wettonmill car park or Grindon (car park/picnic area at the top end of the village, infrequent bus service and also Postbus from Leek).*

After a climb to Grindon, a long section of old packhorse route through the hills is followed by a similar length of easy valley walking in the erratic company of the river Manifold.

❺ Stone arched Weag's Bridge straddles the river Manifold where the narrow road crosses the former Leek & Manifold Light Railway. At this point the river is, in summer, normally already subterranean, though we shall the real thing later in the walk. **At the very junction on the Grindon side of the bridge, a stile sends a faint path steeply climbing the pasture, a nature reserve of Staffordshire Wildlife Trust. It rises with the fence on the left to a pair of gates giving access to the road.** Look back to see a fair prospect of the Manifold Valley, featuring Beeston Tor above the confluence with the Hamps.

Cross straight over the road for a pointless short-cut of the hairpin bend, and rise a little further as far as a bridle-gate on the left. Though the road leads more quickly into Grindon, this presents a more

pleasant option. Go left with the wall, dropping into a dry valley. Turn right up the wallside, and maintain this course up the fading, broadening side valley. Grindon's church spire appears as a guide, and the way rises towards it. Bear left of the farm ahead, crossing a couple of stiles to join a farm lane. Go left and keep on as it becomes a footway only, rising to a T-junction with a rough lane. Go right to enter the village, and left up past the old school to the pub.

Grindon is a peaceful village a breezy thousand feet up. A nice little green sits outside the mid-19th century All Saints church, its very tall spire is a major local landmark. Outside the church gate is the Rindle Stone, its wording informing *The Lord of the Manor of Grindon established his rights to this rindle at the Stafford Assizes the 17 March 1802*. Rindle is Anglo-Saxon for rivulet, and refers to a claim on the intermittent stream flowing through the village. The *Cavalier Inn* dates originally from the mid-17th century.

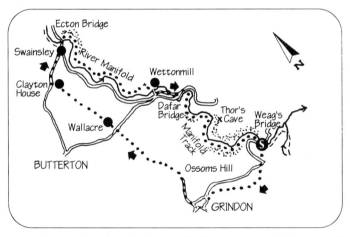

Bear right to the church, above which a narrow cul-de-sac road heads away from the small car park, dropping down through the fields. This is the start of our section of old packway, linking Waterfall to the south with Warslow further north. At once there are grand views ahead, up the Manifold Valley with Revidge above Warslow village, and Ecton and Wetton Hills over to the right. Further right is the impressive crag of Thor's Cave, with Wetton village on the hillside behind.

Turn off the road at the point where the tarmac ends and paths come in on either side. From the stile on the left, cross the field to a stile in the hedge in the dip below. Ahead, the deep sided valley of Hoo Brook is outspread, with Butterton up above it to the left, its spire prominent as ever, backed by high moorland. **Continue to drop down the forming hollow, largely with a hedge for company, to arrive at a footbridge and path junction on Hoo Brook.**

Across the bridge turn downstream through a stile to a tiny bridge on a tiny spring, then bear left up the hedge-side out of the valley. For a direct route to Wettonmill, simply continue downstream. **On the brow we pass Broadmeadow Farm over to the left, and a camping barn to the right.** Beyond, Ecton and Wetton Hills are impressively arrayed across the Manifold Valley. **Keep straight on the field-sides to emerge onto the narrow Butterton-Wetton road.**

Cross straight over the road and head away. Drop down to the left of Wallacre Farm, over its drive and continue down the field-sides. After two further fields bear left to a bridle-gate in the descending wall. Contour across to a tiny stream with a similarly tiny gate behind, and head up the hedge-side away. Continue straight on, a house appearing ahead. The path quickly merges into a drive, following this out past Clayton House onto another minor road, from Butterton to Ecton. The old packhorse way, meanwhile, continues straight across for Warslow, now as a holloway.

This time turn right along the road, quickly descending past Swainsley Farm and Hall to Ecton Bridge on the Manifold. During this descent the copper spire of Radcliffe's Folly is prominent ahead under Ecton Hill (see WALK 1), while down to our left is the substantial valley of Warslow Brook. Just before the river we pass over a tunnel of the valley road. From here to Wettonmill the line of the old railway was taken over by the valley road, which though used by tourist traffic is for some reason designated as the Manifold Track; the route we take is on the original, now traffic-free road, and is far superior. For more on the old railway, please refer to page 12.

Cross the bridge to a road junction and turn right along the narrow road, at times little more than a rough lane. This runs for almost 1½ miles to Wettonmill. This old road rises and falls and enjoys grand scenery: the Manifold makes a delightful companion, all the more so because beyond Wettonmill it will disappear underground. At the outset we see the big house at Swainsley across the river, and pass an attractive dovecote on the riverbank. The Wetton Hills rise increasingly grandly up ahead.

On passing the drive to Dale Farm the old road quickly reaches Wettonmill Bridge. The limestone knob of Nan Tor on the left secretes a dark hole which has revealed evidence of occupation by Mesolithic man after the departure of the last Ice Age 10,000 years ago. At Wettonmill is a National Trust tearoom and toilets: this delectable spot centred on the proud arched bridge is a visitor honeypot.

Wettonmill Bridge

Cross Wettonmill Bridge to a road junction. Two roads go left, downdale, one direct (modern road on old railway, still) and one crossing a ford on Hoo Brook before meandering off. Either can be taken as they quickly merge a little further, just after the old road crosses Dafar Bridge. Look back to see the craggy knoll of Nan Tor rising above Wettonmill; ahead meanwhile is the first glimpse of Thor's Cave. During this spell the river normally sinks below ground, in amongst some fine limestone cliff scenery.

Where the roads merge go straight ahead on the old railway, now completely traffic-free as it crosses the river on a wooden bridge. The valley bends tightly and regularly as the impressive cliff of Thor's Cave appears ahead. This is visited in WALK 4. **Striding on, it is but another mile to Weag's Bridge.**

$$\boxed{4}$$

THOR'S CAVE

START *Grindon*   *Grid ref. SK 085544*

DISTANCE *6 miles*

ORDNANCE SURVEY MAPS
1:50,000
Landranger 119 - Buxton, Matlock & Dove Dale
1:25,000
Outdoor Leisure 24 - Peak District, White Peak

ACCESS *Start from the village centre. There is a car park/picnic area at the top end of the village. Infrequent bus service and also Postbus from Leek.*

A double crossing of the Manifold Valley, featuring two attractive villages and a wealth of limestone features.

⬤ A breezy thousand feet up, Grindon is a peaceful village high above the Manifold. Its main features are the *Cavalier Inn* and the church with its proud spire: please refer to WALK 3 for more detail. **From the car park entrance descend the side road down the front of the church. After a row of houses and a single one (bearing an 1854 datestone), turn left on a short-lived rough lane. Into the field, advance with a crumbling wall, then keep straight on through the field centre.** Ahead, already, are extensive views further up the Manifold. Down to the right is Thor's Cave with Wetton on the ridge behind.

Keep straight on, down to a trickling stream and up to a stile in front. Bear gently left across the field top to a corner stile onto a farm road. Ahead now is the similarly impressive spire of Butterton church, with the moorland of Revidge rising behind. **Go right down this to a fork, then left towards Ossoms Hill Farm.**

Without entering, the path is signed to the right, (not as per map) passing above the buildings at a gate/stile and contouring through a couple of fields to the top of a steeper open bank. Glorious views lead over Hoo Brook to Butterton still backed by Revidge, a delightful, pastoral landscape. **The thin trod is intermittently waymarked along this flank of Ossoms Hill.** The only greenery is some hawthorn scrub, not the woodland suggested on the map.

Turning the corner the path begins a gentle decline. The views however are still on a high: ahead, the Wetton Hills overlook a scene of great loveliness, enclosing Dale Farm beneath the Sugarloaf - this is to be our route. **The thin path descends through scrub to a stile in a rising fence. Drop left to a footbridge onto a narrow road. Advance to the junction in front and cross Wettonmill Bridge to Wetton Mill.**

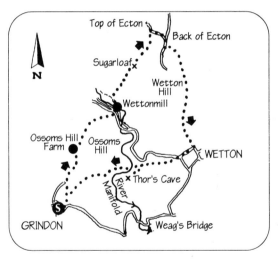

Here the National Trust has a little tearoom and toilets. With the Manifold gliding through, this delectable spot centred on the proud arched bridge is a visitor honeypot. Here too we cross over the line of the Manifold Track, the old railway running in tandem with the minor valley road; indeed, there is a something of an identity crisis in this section - see WALK 3. Just downstream from here the happy river is to be drawn underground, leaving, in normal summer conditions, a dry and stony bed for the ensuing five miles to Ilam.

Across the bridge take the lane rising away to Dale Farm. On starting out, immediately above is a cave lurking in the limestone knob of Nan Tor, and a stile gives access to investigate the dark hole which has revealed evidence of occupation by Mesolithic man not long after the departure of the last Ice Age 10,000 years ago.

Head straight up the farmyard and out on a track into a deep hollow. The limestone bluff known as the Sugarloaf guards its head. Just beneath it the track swings away, leaving a footpath to climb beneath the rock. Behind it a stile is reached into a corner of scrub woodland, but the path strides a corner to another stile back out, and heads away outside the wooded bank. At the end cross to the other side of the wall and continue up, a track forming to meet a narrow road serving Top of Ecton. Here also is a charming dewpond. Just ahead is Broad Ecton Farm.

Turn right up to the brow. Here we are greeted by a prospect of big limestone pastures at the back of the Wetton Hills. **Drop down to a junction and then sharp left. At the first house at Back of Ecton contour back above the wall (through trees) to find a stile on the left in the corner. Slant right down the centre of the field to the bottom corner, where a stile admits onto the National Trust's Wetton Hills. Cross to the dry stream and bear right up the pasture, a broadening green path slanting to a wall corner and thence up the brow.**

From a fence-stile at the top bear left to another, then the path slants up round the brow and away to a stile in the wall at the end. The NT sign now describes Wetton Hill in the singular! Here there are good views to Thor's Cave and across to Grindon dominated by its spire. Wetton village also appears just ahead. **The path drops down through an old quarry to join a rough lane just in front, which runs down into Wetton village. Go left if seeking refreshment, right for the route.** If visiting the *Royal Oak*, which stands back from an attractive junction, a footpath through the churchyard short-cuts back onto the route. See page 17 for more on Wetton.

Head along the lane to the junction at the edge of the village, and keep on the descending Wettonmill road. Very quickly, after a rough lane, take a stile on the left. Head down the field centre, a hollow forming to lead down to a stile into scrubby slopes. Just before, the dark hole of Thor's Cave is prominent on the limestone knoll up to the left, with Grindon church spire ahead.

Down through the scrub a branch path left leads along and then up steps to Thor's Cave. Dark holes penetrate the limestone cliff in this remarkable spot some 60ft in height. Care is needed on the worn limestone at the entrance, and also if peering out of the narrow slit of the West Window. The cave has yielded evidence of occupation by Palaeolithic man, around 12,000 years ago in the latter stages of the last Ice Age. The outstanding view looks far up the Manifold Valley.

Returning to the path, it drops down to a footbridge over the dry river onto the Manifold Track. Cross straight over to a stile and a path heads up into a little undergrowth. Rise up the fieldside to a stile. Here look back to appraise Thor's Cave from a fresh angle. **A superb path contours around through the woods, curving into the side valley to arrive at a corner stile. Rising into a field, don't cross the trickle on the left but follow it to a stile at the top. A path runs to cross the stream, thence steeply up to rejoin the outward route just short of Grindon.**

Thor's Cave: looking up the Manifold Valley from the entrance

5

WATERFALL & THE HAMPS

START *Grindon* *Grid ref. SK 085544*

DISTANCE *5¾ miles*

ORDNANCE SURVEY MAPS
1:50,000
Landranger 119 - Buxton, Matlock & Dove Dale
1:25,000
Outdoor Leisure 24 - Peak District, White Peak

ACCESS *Start from the village centre. There is a car park/picnic area at the top end of the village, above the church. Infrequent bus service and also Postbus from Leek.*

A dip into the wooded Hamps Valley to trace a section of the Manifold Track. After the village of Waterfall a contrastingly open return is made. More tarmac than most walks, though almost exclusively on traffic-free byways and lanes. For more on Grindon, see WALK 3.

S From the car park take the road down into the village, and from the junction by the *Cavalier* pub descend the road past the various village paraphernalia (bus shelter, seat, phone, postbox, notice board) and the old school. After Porch Farm turn right past the White House, then leave this rough lane by a walled footway down to the left. A broader track merges, after which take a stile on the right. Slant across the fields to the rear of the farm buildings at Buckfurlong, and down the steadily forming hollow.

The way runs down through several stiles as a dry valley takes shape, passing a grass-filled dewpond at a farm track and down more pleasantly to another dry dewpond. From here drop more steeply

through a wooded hollow. Before long escape left from this onto a grassy shelf, then curve down the left side of a knoll to approach the Manifold Track on the valley bottom. Turn right parallel with it to join it at a gate by a bridge on the Hamps under Old Soles Wood.

The Hamps is an enigmatic river, for after abandoning the National Park at Winkhill and looking set for lower country, it makes a significant about-turn. Re-entering at Waterhouses it enjoys a snaking course through a deep wooded valley before joining the Manifold at Beeston Tor, back in the thick of the action. In practise, it disappears at Waterhouses and re-appears a few feet from the Manifold at Ilam, having taken a more direct subterranean course under the hills.

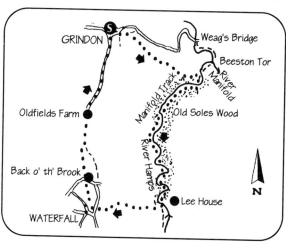

Turn right along the surfaced way of the former railway for a long mile and a half. This winds entirely pleasurably through a deep-sided, wooded valley, though the combination of surfaced rail track and dry river is also rather bizarre! Although the old railway takes the name of the Manifold, for half of its course it actually follows the unsung Hamps. The Manifold Track is featured in greater detail in WALK 1.

After umpteen crossings of the dry river the enclosing slopes relent. With a footbridge and possible refreshments at Lee House on the left and Sparrowlee Farm on the knoll ahead, take a kissing-gate on the right. Follow this small side valley away, tracing the normally dry stream for a good half-mile until reaching a single stone slab footbridge. Cross to a stile up behind it and rise up the field to the wall at the top. On the left is the well named knoll of Pike Low.

From the wall corner, with the houses of Waterfall ahead, take a stile in the corner just behind and cross an enclosure to a stile onto a narrow road in Waterfall. If omitting the village centre, go right and enter the churchyard. To encompass the village, cross straight over the road, along past farm buildings and on to a gap-stile in front of a house. Go left on the short lane out to a junction and a tiny green.

This charming little corner is the heart of Waterfall. It sports both village pump and old stocks, phone box and seat. An attractive red brick house stands back from it. Double back along the road to the right just as far as the *Red Lion* pub. From a stile on the right by a house, advance to another just behind it and cross to the churchyard, entering by a stile. The rather austere looking parish church of St. James & St. Bartholomew dates from 1792.

From a stile in the bottom left corner of the churchyard drop down to another below. Bear left down to a footbridge over a pond (an attractive corner) and a stile onto the road in front of a large house at Back o' th' Brook. This area is changed somewhat from the map. Go left a few yards to a stile on the right, and onto a rough track just above. Go right between house and modern barn, then turn up the side of the barn and escape by rising with the hedge on the left. Looking back, Waterfall is overtopped by the vast quarry site at Cauldon Low, with its main building resembling Mission Control, Houston. Further to the right is the mast-topped Ipstones Edge.

Passing old mine workings, a wall takes over and leads on towards the wooded knoll of Grub Low. Prominent over to the right is the more impressive tumulus site on Waterfall Low. At old, small-scale quarry workings just short of Grub Low, bear right to a stile in the wall to meet the head of an enclosed, part hollowed bridleway. This was a packhorse route linking Waterfall to Warslow by way of Grindon. Go left with the wall and the briefly faint track reforms to run on to Oldfields Farm. The 18th century house boasts an impressive, three-storey frontage. Head away on its surfaced drive, this lane leading directly back to Grindon, emerging adjacent to the pub. The church spire soon appears ahead, while there are fine views over rolling country to the west, towards the moorland ridge of Morridge.

6

BUTTERTON &
GRINDON MOORS

START Onecote   Grid ref. SK 049551

DISTANCE 6¼ miles

ORDNANCE SURVEY MAPS
1:50,000
Landranger 119 - Buxton, Matlock & Dove Dale
1:25,000
Outdoor Leisure 24 - Peak District, White Peak

ACCESS Start from the village centre. Parking in the vicinity of the village hall (former school) just off the B5053. Served by Postbus from Leek and Hartington-Longnor-Leek Wednesday market bus. An alternative start is Butterton, with a good sized lay-by at the western end.

A grand ramble in colourful, unfrequented country.

S Onecote (pronounced On-cut) is a tiny, unassuming village on the Hamps, its features ranged along the arms of a T-junction. St. Luke's church dates from 1755, in a cramped location pressed up against a farmyard. There is a Primitive Methodist Chapel of 1822, while the homely *Jervis Arms* is named after one of Nelson's aides at Trafalgar.

Leave the T-junction by the side road past the church, and after a few minutes fork right down the drive to Onecote Grange. Bear right to the farm, passing between barns and the big house to rise away on an enclosed track. Emerging into a field it immediately joins a farm road to Mixon: remain on this for a good mile. This unsung corner of the Hamps' upper reaches reveals some splendid ox-bow formations as the stream meanders between scrubby flanks. My winter's stroll also disclosed a lone deer stag and more than one heron.

When the drive to Mixon Grange turns off, advance on the track towards Mixon Mine. Approaching the farm, turn down to the right before the first building, immediately after the plantation. A track drops down into the site of the former mine, slowly being reclaimed by nature. The path doubles back down to the right, through the trees to a stile, then across two fields down to a footbridge on the trickling Hamps. Bear right up the bank to a stile on the brow, then go left with the fence, aiming for the farm at Black Brook. After an intervening gate bear right to cut a corner, taking a small gate just past a kink in the fence to join a rough track leading into the yard.

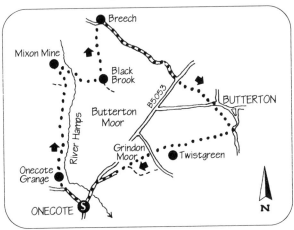

Go left of the house and head upstream with a tiny brook, which is soon crossed to a stile. Bear left to a stile ahead, up a little bank and head away across archetypal open scrub country. Always gently rising, bear left to shadow a small watercourse along the top edge of the pasture, ultimately crossing a couple of field-tops towards the farmhouse at Breech, emerging onto a narrow farm access road. Ahead are grand views to the heathery moorland of Revidge, the upper valley of Warslow Brook, and the high moorland of Merryton Low and Morridge up at its head.

Go right on this meandering road along the crest of the hill and down to New Hillhouse Farm. The walk's highest point offers further sweeping views, particularly when dropping down the other side - beyond Butterton church spire (and Grindon's to its right) backed by the Wetton Hills. At the farm note the oval stone *Thomas & Margaret Salt 1868* on the front. **Advance to Hayes Farm and turn right, remaining on the road which drops then rises to meet the B5053.**

Cross to a stile and head down the field-side. At the end take care not to leap into the spring before resuming with the infant Hoo Brook for company and the church spire beckoning. The way is deflected by a wall to a corner stile, then down again with Bolland's Hall to the right. Just short of the end locate a gap-stile in the wall corner, and down to a gate onto a little lane and out onto the road on the edge of Butterton.

To visit the village centre (shop, pub, church, tearoom - see also WALK 1) go left along the road, and leave by descending the Grindon road to the right to the ford at the foot of the village. An alternative way to the foot of the village goes left for only 60 yards, then turn down a short drive after the first house. Take a stile on the left in front of the cottage at the end, and turn downstream again with Hoo Brook. Follow its right bank down through several stiles until reaching a row of cottages. A tiny footbridge crosses to them, then down a little footway and out onto the road by a ford. The tearoom is just a minute up to the left.

This is a truly charming corner as the brook crosses the little road, a footway alongside Brookside Cottage saving the risk of wet feet. Immediately after the cottage turn right again, up its yard to a short flight of steps and equally short enclosed footway. In the field turn left along the wall-side, and keep on to a gap-stile at the end. This is the first of a string of stiles and gates leading gradually upstream. Just after passing along the front of a house (The Twist), a confluence is reached. Cross to the barns behind, and a tractor track climbs away. Rising to the brow, pass through a couple of gates to the right of Twistgreen Farm. Look back to savour a fine prospect: left of Butterton church spire are Warslow and Revidge, and to the right are the rounded Ecton and Wetton Hills.

Absorbing the farm drive continue out onto a road and cross to the National Trust's pocket upland of Grindon Moor. A thin path heads off through all too brief heather. Across it the path descends through mixed terrain, passing left of a ruin and down to a stile onto a rough lane. Descend this past Home Farm and out onto the B5053 again. Go left for five minutes to finish. En route we pass an old milestone, also look back left up to the two gabled front of Onecote Hall.

7

RAMSHAW ROCKS

START *The Mermaid* Grid ref. SK 036604

DISTANCE *7½ (or 6) miles*

ORDNANCE SURVEY MAPS
1:50,000
Landranger 119 - Buxton, Matlock & Dove Dale
1:25,000
Outdoor Leisure 24 - Peak District, White Peak

ACCESS *Start from the Mermaid pub on Morridge. There is reasonable parking on the verge opposite and off the side road: the pub car park is for patrons only. Served by Wednesday market day bus to Leek from Hartington and Longnor. An alternative start from the Winking Man on the A53 (GR 026637) carries the Buxton-Leek bus service.*

Rough moorland is the dominant feature of this walk with a memorable objective. A shorter finish avoids the rough section. There's also opportunity for a high altitude pub crawl!

S The *Mermaid* is a remote hostelry at a junction of moorland roads on Morridge. At an altitude of 1460ft/445m it is the fifth highest in England, on a par with the Lake District's *Kirkstone Pass Inn*. **At the end of the pub car park a stile and gate see a track off down the rough pasture.** Though we are immediately within Upper Hulme military training range, the 'danger area' is not entered at any stage.

From the outset the westward views are superb, looking past the impressive beacon to the serrated profiles of Hen Cloud, the Roaches and Ramshaw Rocks. **The track descends, at times faintly but with a fence close by on the right. When track and fence coverge at a stream coming in from the left, continue straight down the near side of the stream, somewhat just above its increasingly deep confines.**

A path forms and spirals down to a confluence. Cross the right-hand stream, and from the gate behind it a track rises away. Quickly fading, simply head up towards the barn. To its right is a gate, from where a grassy farm track runs along to Little Swainsmoor Farm. Pass between the buildings and out along the drive to Swainsmoor Farm. Do likewise, but on leaving forsake the drive at the first bend and head across the large pasture, slanting down to the far corner.

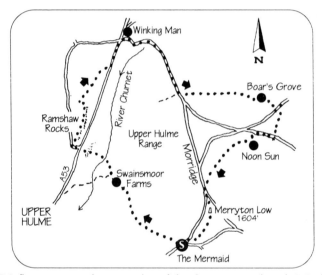

Briefly we are on the very edge of the danger area, though it is the aggressive skyline of Ramshaw Rocks, ahead, that demands undivided attention. **At the end turn down a forming track to cross a sidestream and gate, and over the mini brow behind to find a distinctive single-slab footbridge on the main stream.** This is the infant river Churnet, within a mile and a half of its birth.

From a stile just behind, rise up the wallside. Ignore a branch left part way up, and go to the top where a stile admits to a slim plantation. Looking back, the *Mermaid* is little more than a speck on the skyline above the colourful country of the military range. **Up through the trees we emerge with Ramshaw Rocks impressively looming just above. A stile above points the way up two small fields (passing a walled spring in the second) onto the A53 at Rocks Bar.**

Cross straight over the main road to the cottage and up the side road just as far as the brow. This tract of heather moor on which the Ramshaw Rocks repose is in the hands of the National Park Authority, and there is open access to walkers subject to closure at times of high fire risk. Hen Cloud and the Roaches re-appear on this brow.

Turn right on the main path rising towards the rocks, a shapely pinnacle being the first of interest. With occasional variants and branches the path rises past the lower grouping to the major rocks ahead. The path keeps to the 'back' of the rocks, though there are numerous tempting diversions to explore, with care, the many nooks and crannies. This is splendid stuff, the uniformly angled rocks resulting in stupendous overhangs above bouldery heather slopes. Though different in character, these tilted rocks share their origins with the nearby Roaches. **The highest point is soon attained, and a grand place to be.** The view features much of our walk; the adjacent Roaches and Hen Cloud, of course; and to the north, Shutlingsloe and Shining Tor.

Resume north on the rapidly fading ridge and outcrops. At a wall corner just below, a thin path runs left with the wall to another corner, then right to leave the access area at a path junction. Turn right on the narrow sunken way, still in the heather. It swings left more broadly then turns right to become enclosed as it prepares to leave the moor.

Here take a thin trod left for a few yards along the fence side. At a stile we too leave the moor, and slant across to the wall opposite. Go left to its end, and on to a gate in the fence ahead. A converted chapel stands by the main road just down to the right. **Head away alongside a fence, through rough pasture curving right and up to a gate back onto the A53 opposite some barns at Stake Gutter.**

Go left, making grateful use of the broad verges for a few minutes as far as a junction. Just before it, note the old milestone (*Buxton 7, Leek 5*). **Turn right on the Warslow road, at once passing the rear of the *Winking Man* pub.** Named after a rock feature on Ramshaw, at 1450ft/442m this is the seventh highest pub in England. Four of these are claimed by Staffordshire, with the *Royal Cottage*, fourth highest, just along the main road. **This easy road walk lasts for about a mile.** Curving round the ravine-like head of the Churnet, enjoy grand views back over it to the jagged profile of Ramshaw Rocks.

On a brow, with a road fork just ahead, a military access track goes off to the right. The easy option keeps straight on the road and its improving verges to rejoin the circuitous route as it comes in at the following junction, just short of Merryton Low. **Those feeling adventurous can branch left opposite the military track, on a contrastingly faint trod through the heather. As this rapidly fades, there is little point in seeking it out!**

Stride purposefully down the heathery slope, the objective being a distinct confluence at the lower point of the moor, due east. Cross the fence here to leave the moor for rough pasture. Continue downstream with a crumbling wall to another confluence. The grassy bank by a ruin and occasional trees makes an attractive spot for a break amid unfrequented country.

Crossing the right branch a well sunken way rises through forlorn gateposts, and is traced up to the brow where it fades. Keep straight on through a crumbling wall and alongside another, with the farm-

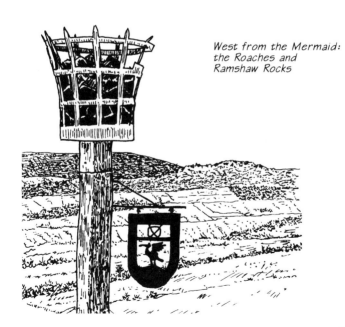

West from the Mermaid: the Roaches and Ramshaw Rocks

house at Boars Grove just ahead. The track re-forms to slant down over a stream and up into the yard. Simply continue away on the drive, rising back onto heather moor to meet a road. There are good views north-east to Chrome Hill rising above its fellow limestone knolls. **Go left for a couple of minutes, and before the road drops away past a car park, double back right into more pathless heather. This spell is briefer: rising past a stake, slant across to an obvious gap-stile in a rising wall.**

Cross two fields to the farm at Round Knowl ahead, a stile admitting onto the road. Go right, soon returning to open moor, with the Merryton Low/Morridge skyline ahead. Before a junction take the first branch left, down a farm drive to Noon Sun. At the first buildings branch right on a fenced track, swinging left with it down to a minor brook. On crossing, take a fence-stile just above and head up the field by a sike. Maintain this course through stiles in rougher pasture, rising increasingly pleasantly with a fence to arrive beneath a ruined barn. Take the stile in front and bear left through newly planted alien trees. From a stile in the fence at the end, rise the few yards to another stile onto the broad verge of the Morridge road.

The road is joined just short of a junction. Cross to look down upon Blake Mere. This grand scene recalls the legend of a mermaid who lured men into the pool, hence its alternative name of Mermaid Pool. What is more certain is that it provides a fine foreground to our erstwhile skyline back across the A53. **At the road fork, take a path straight ahead to the Ordnance Survey column (2989) on Merryton Low.** This triangle of open country is also owned by the National Park Authority and open to walkers.

At 1604ft/489m Merryton Low is the summit of the walk. It is also the highest point on the many miles of Morridge, being overtopped only by Oliver Hill above Flash, where it meets Axe Edge. The extensive panorama features particularly big views south-east, with moorland sloping down to Revidge. Not surprisingly, however, the highlight probably remains the closer features to the west: from here, Ramshaw Rocks are somewhat overshadowed by the Roaches. Affixed to the trig. point is a local regiment's war memorial. **Leave by the thinner path south, forging on alongside a low bank to reach a fence corner. At this point the *Mermaid* returns to view just ahead. Drop down to it to finish, possibly for well-earned refreshment.**

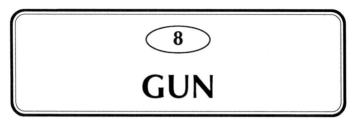

8

GUN

START *Meerbrook*   *Grid ref. SJ 987608*

DISTANCE *4¾ miles*

ORDNANCE SURVEY MAPS
1:50,000
Landranger 118 - Stoke-on-Trent & Macclesfield
1:25,000
Outdoor Leisure 24 - Peak District, White Peak

ACCESS *Start from the village centre. There is a large lay-by outside the village hall on the main road west of the pub. Served by extremely infrequent bus from Leek.*

An easy walk with the modest but delectable heathery summit of Gun dividing pleasant fieldpaths and tracks.

S Meerbrook is an unassuming little community on the National Park boundary. It consists largely of a pub, the *Lazy Trout*, a youth hostel and the parish church of St. Matthew. Most visitors come for the Tittesworth Reservoir amenities just along the road (see WALK 9). **From the hall head west up the road out of the village, and within 100 yards take a stile on the left. Head along the fieldside, on through a gate and briefly enclosed past some farm buildings at Alder Lee. From the stile in front cross to a rickety plank footbridge, and on to a gateway across the corner immediately behind. Cross the field to a footbridge on a deep little brook, then turn up the field-side.**

Already there are good views back to the Roaches and the particularly impressive little peak of Hen Cloud. **This same line is maintained, slanting across several field tops. Part way on, cross the foot of an enclosed track to an old gap-stile in front, then resume as before. At the top a stile admits onto a farm lane. Go right along the drive to**

Gunside, keeping left on the track above the buildings. Here the ways fork: take the left branch climbing to a gate into a field. A green track heads away, bearing right and running on past an old quarry and slanting pleasantly up the field past a stand of trees.

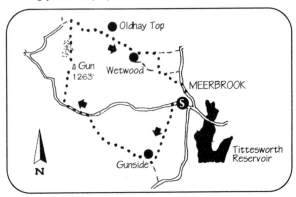

Over to the right the extended view embraces Ramshaw Rocks slotted in between the Roaches and Hen Cloud, while ahead Gun's heathery crown makes itself known. **On reaching a gate the track becomes fainter. Keep straight on to another gate in the wall ahead, then on past a small stand of Scots pine, tracing and crossing a ditch to a corner gate. Another track is joined and leads across to a gate onto a road beneath the moor. Turn left up the road, already virtually at its brow.** The lush bilberry verge has fine open views down to the left.

Just yards short of the top take a stile on the right by an old gateway with a benchmark. A smashing path runs on through the heather for the gentle climb to the waiting Ordnance Survey column (S2615), passing a standing stone (benchmark again) on the way.

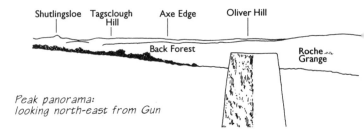

Peak panorama:
looking north-east from Gun

At a very modest 1263ft/385m this grassy knoll amongst heather and bilberry is a super spot. It is even an unsung 'Marilyn', one of only four tops in the National Park to rise more than 500ft/150m above their surrounds: a feat not even the Roaches nor Shutlingsloe can manage. The extensive view is also something to be proud of. Southwards are Tittesworth Reservoir and Leek; westwards the Cloud and Sutton Common mast see the Cheshire Plain receding into the distance. The more interesting panorama is illustrated below.

The path resumes north, dropping down to follow a crumbling wall, then on between old walls as a fine old cart way and past a wood on the left. Emerging, classic open moorland leads delectably on down a better defined 'ridge'. The path drops to a concrete farm road by some sheep pens. Turn right, over a cattle-grid and into contrastingly dull pastures. At a fork at a wood corner, turn down to the left, the drive descending to the farm at Oldhay Top. Throughout this descent there are grand views over the broad valley to the Roaches skyline.

At the bend just above the farm, drop right to a stile and down to a wall-stile below. Slant down the large field to the trees in the corner, passing into them look for a stile at a trickle on the right. Through the hedge, turn down onto a rough farm track. Go right a short way but before the gate and farm buildings of Wetwood drop left to a stile in the hedge, joining another concrete farm drive. Turn down here to a path crossroads at the second cattle-grid. Here go right on a firm track, quickly reaching another path crossroads. One could keep straight on here to emerge onto the road just above the village hall.

At this crossroads take the branch bearing left, and as it swings left in the field centre cross to a stile opposite. From it bear left to a gate onto a road and go right to re-enter Meerbrook. If not seeking the pub then turn first right on a narrow, unsigned back lane, winding round past the rear of the church to return directly to the village hall.

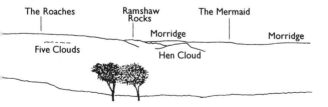

43

9

THE ROACHES

START *Meerbrook*   *Grid ref. SJ 993603*

DISTANCE *7½ miles*

ORDNANCE SURVEY MAPS
1:50,000
Landranger 118 - Stoke-on-Trent & Macclesfield
Landranger 119 - Buxton, Matlock & Dove Dale
1:25,000
Outdoor Leisure 24 - Peak District, White Peak

ACCESS *Start from the Severn-Trent car park at Tittesworth Reservoir on the eastern edge of Meerbrook. On weekends between Spring and Autumn a 'Park & Ride' scheme operates to the Roaches where parking is extremely limited. The main road at Upper Hulme is served by Buxton-Leek express buses.*

One of Peakland's most famous features visited by a route from the valley that offers a leisurely, more appreciative approach.

S The water company operates a visitor centre at the car park, with information, nature trails and refreshments. **Return to the road and turn right.** Immediately, the Roaches and Hen Cloud grace the skyline ahead. **Just short of the first buildings (Middle Hulme) take a stile on the left and head up the field. Towards the top a stile on the right gives access to a rough lane. Turn up here as far as a sharp bend to the left.**

Don't be confused if the map and the actual route seem at variance at this point. **Take the stile in front and rise up the field to a little gateway giving access to the now initially sunken and abandoned old way. Cross straight over it to a stile then head up the field outside the holloway. This fades but the way runs on towards the barns ahead.**

At a stile/gate just before the barns a concession path saves us from the worst excesses of the farmyard. Turn left, wallside, up to another stile, then right on a rough track towards the farm. Stay on this above all the buildings to emerge onto a road in Upper Hulme. Go right, down past an engineering works to a hairpin bend in the village. The bridge, ford and cottages here make a pleasing scene. Just up to the right is *Ye Olde Rock Inn*, a tiny Methodist Church (the former Sunday School of 1838) and the A53 Buxton-Leek road.

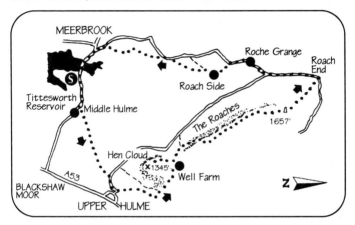

Our route goes straight up the concrete drive from the bridge. This becomes a track running on with the brook to the forlorn remains of Dains Mill. Continue up behind it and a path runs upstream. Ahead, Ramshaw Rocks (see WALK 7) appear in impressive style, contrasting with the modest outcrops immediately above our path. **Turn sharp left on a green path immediately after the minor rocks above our path, to find a stile. Rise to another grassy path and left onto a farm drive. Go right on this up the field to Well Farm.** Leaving the trees behind, the Roaches' southernmost rocks appear impressively above the farm. Ramshaw Rocks still look very aggressive also.

Approaching the yard take a stile on the left to circumvent the farm environs, and from a stile at the top end we enter the Roaches estate. Though the clear path rises right to a wall-stile beneath the Roaches, to visit Hen Cloud rise left with the wallside to join a clear path by a stile on the dividing saddle. The detour onto Hen Cloud is short and quickly accomplished, a direct climb left onto the well defined top.

It is worth every moment to savour the situation of this grand little peak. The 1345ft/410m summit is perfectly placed on the crest of the highest rocks. This 100ft buttress offers over 100 climbing routes, a popular second choice to the busy Roaches.

Return down the path to the stile, crossing an island field to a stile onto the foot of the Roaches. Take the broad path left, swinging round to join a drive to Rockhall Cottage. Turn right up this along the front of the cottage. Once a gamekeeper's house it was latterly the home of Doug Moller, self-styled 'Lord of the Roaches'. More recently it has been restored and operates as a climbing hut in memory of the late Don Whillans, a true-grit mountaineering character.

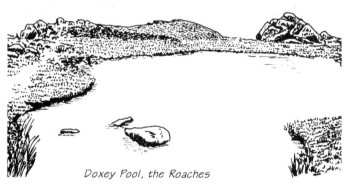

Doxey Pool, the Roaches

At the gateway just beyond turn into the trees and rise to a flight of stone steps. These lead through the lower tier of crags onto a shelf. If there are climbers about then you'll see them in this neck of the woods. This is the major climbing area of the Roaches, with a further 100 routes of up to 100ft: best known perhaps is the Sloth, an alarming overhang first mastered over 40 years ago. **Turn left on the path, savouring the situation of the cliffs above, passing through trees and on to a path junction. This coincides with a major cleft in the rocks, so turn up between them onto the broad edge path. Go left along the crest of the diminishing crags. An obvious halting place is Doxey Pool, an atmospheric sheet of water in a curious setting.**

From here the adjacent edge offers its finest vantage point, back along the buttresses to Hen Cloud. Immediately below, the tops of the Five Clouds are easily identified. Ahead, the Ordnance Survey column marking the Roaches' summit also appears. **Forging on, the path soon**

gains the trig. point (S2596) on its eroded crest. At 1656ft/505m this is the second highest hill in Staffordshire, overtopped only by Oliver Hill, above Flash. To the north the Back Forest ridge (see WALK 11) looks stunted from this lofty spot, while Shutlingsloe, more distantly, looks undiminished.

Beyond here the path descends more rapidly to pass some particularly shapely scattered outcrops before the road at Roach End. During this spell enjoy grand views north over Back Forest, moorland and woodland falling to the river Dane. Since 1938 the area has been a home to escaped wallabies from the private zoo of Lt Col Brocklehurst of nearby Swythamley; always difficult to discern, it seems human disturbance has finally rendered them extinct. **Turn left and enjoy a near traffic-free walk on this back road.** The outcrops of the edge are high above, and across the valley is heather-capped Gun (see WALK 8). **At a fork drop right through Roche Grange, a farming hamlet.**

At the second sharp bend after Roche Grange, when the road turns right, take a stile/gate in front and cross the fields towards Roach Side Farm. A rough track is joined at the back of the house. Go right, passing behind the buildings then right again to a stile in the wall heading away. Cross to a gateway beneath horse chestnut trees then head down the field, parallel with the drive. From a stile slant away from the drive, down to a corner stile. With a tree-lined stream on the left, descend two field centres to stiles onto the road at Greenlane.

Go left just around the bend, then take a stile on the left. From one just behind it a faint path crosses the field centre to a stone-slab footbridge. Rise to the wall and on to a corner stile at the end. Go left, briefly enclosed, then after a plank bridge resume along the short fieldside to a farm drive. Almost opposite is another stile, from where cross a sike to a hedge-gap then advance with the tall hedge on the right, persisting with it to the abandoned farm of Lower Lee.

Pass along the other side of the sad ruin and out on its grassy drive onto the road. Go left onto the road through Meerbrook. The *Lazy Trout* pub is impeccably placed on the left, while to the right are a small youth hostel and St. Matthew's church. **Go left down the road to return to the start.** En route we pass the Methodist chapel, and leading over the upper section of the reservoir the upper pool is maintained as a nature conservation area; it also makes a suitable concluding foreground to Hen Cloud and the Roaches.

(**10**)

RIVER DANE

START Danebridge   Grid ref. SJ 964651

DISTANCE 4¾ miles

ORDNANCE SURVEY MAPS
1:50,000
Landranger 118 - Stoke-on-Trent & Macclesfield
1:25,000
Outdoor Leisure 24 - Peak District, White Peak

ACCESS *Start from the road bridge on the river Dane between the hamlets of Danebridge and Wincle. There is parking on the wide section of road as it rises from the bridge towards Wincle. The pub car park is strictly for patrons only. Extremely infrequent bus link from Leek.*

A lovely ramble by a beautiful river and through charming country-side of great beauty, history and character.

❿ Dane Bridge itself is a tall, single-arched sandstone structure. To the south, on the Staffordshire side, the true hamlet of Danebridge comprises of a few select dwellings and a Wesleyan Methodist Chapel of 1834. North of the bridge, in Cheshire, is a slightly more populous group that though part of Wincle is regularly known as Danebridge also. The *Ship Inn* dates from the 16th century and features some mullioned windows.

From the bridge head up towards Wincle, and bear left along the trout farm drive, a concession path which quickly absorbs the public path. The latter leaves the road higher up, after the first group of houses: it descends steps into a field and crosses to join the drive. The lively Dane provides immediate company en route to Danebridge Fisheries, passing a large pond on the right.

At Pingle Cottage the path is channelled between car park and river, quickly emerging beneath a wooded bank. Beyond the next stile as the river swings away, the footpath remains with the bank, rejoining the Dane at a tight bend. This is glorious country, with colourful flanks of woodland, bracken and scrub. The river Dane rises on Axe Edge (see WALKS 15 and 17), and flows an untrammelled course on the westernmost extremity of the National Park. During the course of this walk it marks the boundary between Staffordshire and Cheshire. It joins the Weaver Navigation at Northwich only after a long journey across the Cheshire Plain.

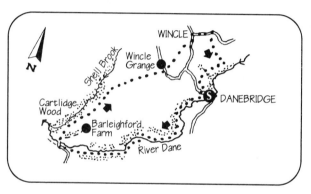

Resume downstream, now keeping faith with the river, passing a weir and reaching a footbridge on the river at the end. Immediately across, turn right on the embanked path alongside a water drain. This conduit takes water from the Dane for canal use by way of Rudyard Reservoir. **Follow this for almost a mile as far as a farm drive just after an earlier stone arched bridge.** Though the calm feeder contrasts strongly with the chirpy Dane, this section still enjoys all the benefits of the adjacent river's surroundings. **At the drive turn down it to Barleigh Ford Bridge.** The redundant ford is just upstream.

At the first bend after the drive leave it for a stile in front. The original path went on up and through Barleighford Farm, but was diverted to this pleasanter course in 1988. **A thin path climbs the wooded bank behind and crosses the centre of the extensive sloping field, aided by some 'Gritstone Way' marker posts.** The deep-cut, well wooded side valley of Shell Brook runs to our left, backed by the slopes of Wincle Minn.

Towards the end the faint path slants to the top, and runs on to a gate/ stile out of the immediate environs of the valley. Over to the right are first glimpses of Hen Cloud and the Roaches. **Continue on the fence side, passing a branch path and on to an old red sandstone barn. Here the path becomes a hollowed characterful old way between trees. Shortly, the Gritstone Way departs at a branch left, but our path continues straight up this classic route to emerge into a field corner.**

Don't take the gate left or the track right, but keep straight on by a line of trees. At the end of the tapering field is a stile, from where the sunken way takes shape again rising to the right. Over the brow it slants down to cross a stream and rises alongside it onto a narrow road at Wincle Grange. The farm was a grange of Combermere Abbey, a Cistercian monastery on the Cheshire-Shropshire border. The splendid sandstone house survives from the late monastic period, and with its impressive barns retains the grange layout.

Turn right just a few yards, and with a pond on the right, take a gate on the left. A green track heads away beneath a wooded knoll. At once a glorious prospect opens out, with the shapely cone of Shutlingsloe to the north. The panorama swings round eastwards to the hills and moors above Wildboarclough and the Dane, the Back Forest ridge featuring the Hanging Stone, the Roaches, Hen Cloud and Gun. **The track heads across the pasture in line for Shutlingsloe. When it fades simply keep on to a corner stile. Slant down to the wall below, and just short of the corner pass through the line of trees and down a hedge side onto a road.**

Go left to the junction (passing the Parsonage and Lane House Farm with mullioned windows) in front of the church and school. St. Michael's church dates from 1647 but was restored in 1882. **Turn right down the Wildboarclough road, and up the other side take a drive on the right opposite Hammerthorn Farm. This runs on then drops steeply to the lone house at Bartomley.**

From a stile in the yard between the buildings go right along the field top, keeping on to drop to a stile into the wooded Hog Clough. A path crosses this and resumes across the next field centre to a path crossroads. For the pub go straight on to a kissing-gate onto a drive then down steps onto the road. **For the bridge, turn left outside the garden wall of the big house, on to a stile then down the steep field to a pair of stiles onto the road by the bridge.**

BACK FOREST

START *Gradbach*   *Grid ref. SJ 999661*

DISTANCE *7¼ miles*

ORDNANCE SURVEY MAPS
1:50,000
Landranger 118 - Stoke-on-Trent & Macclesfield
1:25,000
Outdoor Leisure 24 - Peak District, White Peak

ACCESS *Start from the National Park car park on the cul-de-sac road at Gradbach, just off the Flash-Allgreave road. Extremely infrequent bus link from Leek.*

A walk through the stunning beauty of the Back Forest, where native woodland and rolling moorlands secrete the spectacle of Lud's Church. Some of the paths are concession routes within National Park access land.

⑤ From the car park entrance head right (west) along the narrow cul-de-sac road, and after five minutes turn down the drive to Gradbach Mill, now a youth hostel. During this short opening section the Back Forest ridge, our enchanting objective, is arrayed ahead. Descending the drive we pass a dry well, with stone seats neatly flanking the oval trough.

Impressively restored Gradbach Mill dates from 1785, when it was rebuilt following a fire. Originally a flax mill it later operated as a silk mill then a sawmill. Its large waterwheel was scrapped in the 1950s. After many years of neglect it was bought by the Youth Hostels Association and opened in 1987, one of the best located hostels in the country. Opposite is the mill manager's house, also adapted as part of the hostel.

From the front of the mill resume downstream, to a stile and then down the pasture. At a stile turn into an enclosed pathway. This broadens and as the track doubles back up the hill, take the stile in front and drop down to a footbridge on **Black Brook**, just yards above its confluence with the Dane. This lovely spot is a foretaste of what lies ahead. Here we enter Forest Wood, part of the National Park's Roaches estate, and happily being managed with both wildlife and peaceful recreation in mind.

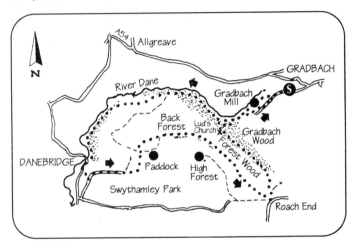

Take the path rising to a guidepost, and then turn right along the level Danebridge path. This runs downstream through the woods, soon rising to a fork where the right branch is taken. Remain on this path for a stunning woodland walk with the river tinkling below. The path works its way largely downhill until emerging from the wood by slanting left up into a field. Keep straight on across to another stile, now with sweeping views over the valley.

Rise to a gorse corner and on, fence side, above a lone house. Cross straight over its drive and maintain a direct line, the path soon re-forming beyond a trickle crossing. Remain on the path from here, contouring on to arrive above the isolated cottage of **Back Dane**. This overlooks the confluence of Clough Brook (from Wildboarclough) with the Dane, while appearing up the side valley is the graceful cone of Shutlingsloe.

Join the rough drive descending to the cottage, but keep straight on the path slanting beyond it. **Entering woodland again the path runs happily on in this quiet corner, leaving the trees at a stile and continuing downstream through a pasture, ultimately merging onto the road at Danebridge.** The bridge itself is a tall, single-arched sandstone structure. If seeking refreshment the *Ship Inn* is two minutes along to the right.

Back Dane,
looking to
Shutlingsloe

Turn left up the road, away from the bridge. On the right is the Wesleyan Methodist Chapel of 1834, still a Methodist church. **Opposite, take a path squeezing up between gardens onto a drive. Go right a short way, then double back left, just a few yards up in front of the house there. Turn right along its front and up to a stile. An old track, now sunken and lost, slants up past farm buildings to rise to a drive at Snipe. Turn left on this hard drive to Park House.**

As the drive contours around the hill we glean super views over Danebridge and across to Shutlingsloe, while just in front the Back Forest ridge takes shape, with the Hanging Stone hovering above. Park House sits on the park wall of Swythamley Hall. The hall itself was once a medieval hunting lodge, burnt down in 1813 and rebuilt in the mid-19th century.

Stay on the drive, past a branch to Hangingstone Farm, to then swing left up towards the farm at Paddock. At a junction at the top is a choice of routes. A footpath rises to a gate and runs on behind the house, rising enclosed to a stile onto the edge of moorland. At a multi-guidepost and estate sign the broad main path rises left to the brow. **A more interesting concession path goes left through the gateway and over a stile above. A path rises then slants across to the Hanging Stone, a monumental gritstone rock.** Affixed are two tablets, one to Lt Col Henry Courtnay Brocklehurst of Swythamley, another to Burke, one of the family's dogs. It was this particular Brocklehurst who founded a private zoo, and descendents of wallabies that escaped in 1938 inhabited this locality until, it seems, recently rendered extinct.

A NOBLE MASTIFF BLACK AND TAN
FAITHFUL AS WOMAN BRAVER THAN A MAN
A GUM AND A RAMBLE HIS HEART AND DESIRE
WITH THE FRIEND OF HIS LIFE THE SWYTHAMLEY SQUIRE

Stone steps climb the far side, and only on peering over the top is the profound drop appreciated! At this very point Shutlingsloe returns to the view in some style, just part of a class panorama with Hen Cloud seen beyond the Roaches.

From the rock top a path heads off through the collapsed wall, swinging right to a stile then on again to a corner stile by sheep pens. Here the 'main' way is joined, a broad track. Go left to the gate/stile in a fence.

*Hanging Stone,
Back Forest*

Here leave the main path by a concession path rising to the right. This runs grandly along the crest of the Back Forest ridge, passing intermittent outcrops in the heather and ultimately gaining the road at Roach End. Ahead, throughout, is the higher level skyline of the Roaches. At one point there is a view down to Gradbach Mill in its glorious surrounds. A branch left at a crossroads offers a short-cut to Lud's Church. The fine section of rebuilt wall on the approach to Roach End is the handiwork of an estate worker who had spent many years down the mines near Stoke-on-Trent: still hard work of course, but what a contrast to be out here day after day in the open air!

Without setting foot on tarmac turn down to the left, on the drive descending towards Lower Roach End. Take an early stile in the wall and a path continues down, now back on the moorland of Back Forest. Quickly becoming stone built this runs down into Arcadian moor-fringe woodland, before delving more deeply into the trees of Forest Wood.

In this shady dell a junction is reached under massive beech trees. Turn left as signed for Lud's Church, and though a little height must be gained initially, this proves to be a splendid path running on through the top edge of the wood. On reaching a fork turn left for Lud's Church. Within 50 yards at another fork go right, quickly reaching the top of the 'church'. Steps descend into the gorge from where a passage is made through its length.

Lud's Church is a magnificent feature, all the more awe-inspiring for its elusive nature. Gritstone walls up to 60ft high line a long, narrow ravine shaped by a distant landslip. Not surprisingly it has its legends, for it is claimed as the Green Chapel, site of an Arthurian duel in the 15th century poem *Sir Gawain and the Green Knight*. Earning more credence perhaps is the theory that it was the 14th century refuge of a religious group known as Lollards, who held services here, hence the 'church'.

Emerging at the front onto the main path again, go left for a minute to a junction at a clearing and the tor-like outcrops of Castle Cliff Rocks. Go right, this good path descending to rejoin the outward route at the footbridge above the confluence. Cross and rise to the stile out of the wood, and unless returning to the hostel turn up the track between small plantations. This same way rises gently through several fields to a house. Entering its yard by a stile go right up onto a narrow road, and turn left along here to finish.

12
WILDBOARCLOUGH

START *Gradbach*   *Grid ref. SJ 999661*

DISTANCE *7 miles*

ORDNANCE SURVEY MAPS
1:50,000
Landranger 118 - Stoke-on-Trent & Macclesfield
1:25,000
Outdoor Leisure 24 - Peak District, White Peak

ACCESS *Start from the National Park car park on the cul-de-sac road at Gradbach, just off the Flash-Allgreave road. Extremely infrequent bus link from Leek.*

A splendid ramble through unfrequented country, largely on old tracks adventuring into the recess of Wildboarclough. Archetypal Western Peak scenery.

⑤ From the car park entrance head right (west) along the narrow road and after five minutes turn down the drive to Gradbach Mill youth hostel. For more on the mill please refer to page 51. **Pass along the front of the mill and over a footbridge on the river Dane.** Though little seen on this walk, the delightful river is a major feature of WALKS 10 and 11.

Enclosed by old walls, a former packhorse and millworkers' path climbs steeply away. Looking back, the mill is well seen in its deep valley setting, while the Roaches rise beyond the Back Forest. **At the top bear left to a gateway, and the green path runs on to the corner. Though the public path goes through the gate and up from the barn to the house above, a concession path climbs straight up the side of the stony pasture. At the top corner go right a few yards to a stile to join the drive, and follow this up onto the road.**

Pause to look back to the Roaches scene, with Ramshaw Rocks slotting in above Gradbach Hill. The lone roadside house here is the Eagle & Child, until 1919 a public house. A splendid and appropriate tablet dated 1738 above the door bears the arms of the Stanleys (Earls of Derby) of Crag Hall, Wildboarclough (illustrated on page 3).

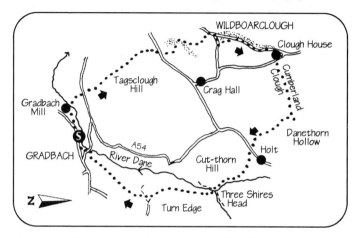

Cross straight over and up the rough lane. This old road emerges into a field and begins an invigorating march over undulating terrain. Views back to the Roaches are replaced by those ahead to Shutlingsloe, appearing as a superb peak, surely at least 2000ft! To the west meanwhile the Cloud and Sutton Common mast appear. **The green road runs grandly on, dropping more steeply at the end as it joins a drive. Ahead the Wildboarclough valley takes deep shape. Cut the bottom corner by dropping right to a stile onto the A54.**

Cross straight over to another stile, and a little path runs to a restored barn. Pass along the front then down to a gate/stile. Cross the field centre then bear left to the far end of the small plantation. The path curves down to a stile at the left end of a wood. In front a magnificent prospect is gleaned as Shutlingsloe rises majestically above the pub in the valley bottom of Wildboarclough. **An old path slants down to the right beneath the wood, opening out at a fork. Here bear left across the field to find a couple of footbridges making life easier. From the corner a path descends, briefly enclosed by walls.**

Here the path splits again. If tempted by the pub, drop straight down to a stile into the trees, narrowly down their side to emerge via a footbridge on attractive Clough Brook onto the road. The pub, the *Crag Inn*, is just yards to the left. Alternatively, turn right along the field to a stile, where an enclosed way runs onto a drive and out to a road in the centre of Wildboarclough. These days this valley name has replaced the name of Crag in references to this hamlet.

From the pub head back along the road to reach the bridge at a road junction. Approaching it we pass the scant remains of Lower Crag Mill, built in 1737 by James Brindley. Born a few miles away on the other side of Buxton, he later came to be recognised as the father of the English canal system. The mill featured three waterwheels atop each other to maximise use of the water supply, which came from a lake in the grounds of 18th century Crag Hall. Standing on the bridge it is difficult to imagine this innocent stream in full fury, yet as recently as 1989 it wreaked havoc here in a spring flood which cost a life and caused the bridge to be rebuilt. **Turn right here up past Crag Mill to the church, absorbing the alcohol-free path.**

Crag Mill is a splendid Georgian building (with working clock), a surprise to find hidden behind the phone box. Dating from 1770, it was the mill manager's house and office to a long departed silk mill, and more recently incorporated the village Post office. It is now a private residence. The simple church of St. Saviour dates from 1904.

Shutlingsloe
across
Wildboarclough

On the near side of the churchyard a byway runs on to a row of cottages incorporating the former school. Keep straight on into the trees and it quickly emerges onto the valley road. Advance in tandem with the clough to approach Clough House. Here take a footbridge on the stream and up the field to the farm. Turn left into the yard and out onto the road, wth a tiny green and a junction up in front.

From the gate up above a fine cart track rises into Cumberland Clough, crossing Cumberland Brook at a footbridge/ford then rising by a colourful wood. Passing beneath the sombre Cumberland Cottage the track rises into the open at a major bend. All this is fine country, with a little waterfall in the clough on the right and Danethorn Hollow up above. Here the Cat & Fiddle path heads off to the left. Keep straight on the main track curving up to the right before easing out. It runs improvingly on to meet the A54 once again.

Cross straight over to a stile and descend to another. Ahead now is upper Dane country. Bear left down the fieldside to meet a green bridleway. Turn right on this to a gate in the corner, then sharply left down the wallside. At the bottom this super way slants right with the wall, down to meet the infant Dane and a footpath. Keep straight on the broad path downstream, by bracken flanks to quickly reach Three Shires Head, a grand spot featured in WALK 17.

Cross both bridges and head away on the broad, gently rising path. Early on, look back down to a little waterfall into a pool. At a gate keep straight on the upper path, soon running grandly on with scattered woodland above. Just past a near-hidden house up above, its drive is joined. Almost at once pass through a gateway on the right and descend a green way past a ruin and lone tree. Ignoring a couple of stiles in the old wall below, cross to a less obvious one in the very corner. Head away with the wall, curving down across a broad track and down to a corner gate/stile.

Bear left across the field to a ladder-stile, then straight down two field centres to meet a wall/hawthorn junction. Head straight down the wallside, maintaining this simple line down a tapering spur (sometimes with a track) to a stile into the yard of a modern house. Go left to its gate onto the road opposite Manor Farm and right down the short hill. Just along to the right is the neat little Gradbach Methodist Chapel of 1849. At the foot of the bank take a stile on the left and head downstream with the Dane. At a confluence with a similar brook cross a footbridge on the latter, and the car park is just yards further along the road to the right.

13

SHUTLINGSLOE

START *Macclesfield Forest*   *Grid ref. SJ 961711*

DISTANCE *5¾ miles*

ORDNANCE SURVEY MAPS
1:50,000
Landranger 118 - Stoke-on-Trent & Macclesfield
1:25,000
Outdoor Leisure 24 - Peak District, White Peak

ACCESS *Start from North West Water's Trentabank car park, east of Langley in the Macclesfield Forest. Langley is served by bus from Macclesfield.*

An easy if steep ascent to a classic summit. A direct return makes this a simple outing, but the full circuit enjoys an extended excursion into the environs of Wildboarclough.

S Macclesfield Forest is spread around and above North West Water's Ridgegate and Trentabank reservoirs, and revives the name of an ancient hunting forest. Opened in 1929, Trentabank Reservoir has a small visitor centre, picnics and forest trails, with a heronry managed by Cheshire Wildlife Trust.

From the centre turn right/east on a short path parallel with the road. It runs to a broad track which immediately sets about climbing into the forest. This firm track soon swings left and runs to a crossroads with a direct climbing path. Turn sharp right on a still broad, firm path that includes steep moments in its climb to the top of the forest.

At a junction keep left to taste respite during a gentler section. Just beyond, at another fork take the path branching right, quickly reaching a stile out of the forest at a guidepost. The old reference to

Shutlingsloe Farm, rather than Shutlingsloe, is a reminder that the route over the summit was only made a public path in 1979. The contrast of open space on leaving the enclosed forest is profound.

Rise away on the largely flagged path, within five minutes gaining a super prospect of our peak, just above. The path runs on to a fence-wall junction stile where the shoulder path runs on left. Our route climbs the wallside to a stile, then a short sharp, pull to the waiting Ordnance Survey column (S2760). At 1660ft/506m this is a spectacular location. A few modest rocks break the surface, while a memorial topograph picks out features of interest. Undoubted highlight is the sudden revelation, only as the trig. point is touched, of the valley of Wildboarclough.

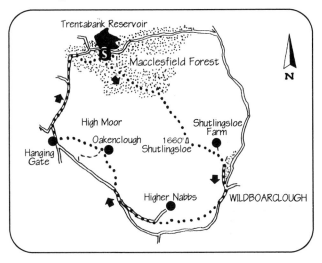

The descent is rapid and, as yellow arrows have been affixed to the trig. point, infallible. A steep descent through rough ground soon transforms into a gentle grassy stroll down the fell. The clear path absorbs the shoulder path and drops down through a couple of stiles, swinging right down with a wall to join a farm drive. Turn right, descending all the way to the road in Wildboarclough. Turn right with the river Dane for just a few seconds to reach the _Crag Inn_. Just along to the left, incidentally, is the hub of Wildboarclough, featuring the church and Crag Mill - see WALK 12.

Immediately after the car park take a stile on the right, and a fine green way slants up the gorse and scrub bank. At the end rise to a wall-stile from where a contouring path heads on through several large fields. Up to the right are glimpses of the bald crown of our erstwhile peak. **Approaching a minor stream the way slants right to cross it, then rises to run on to a stile in the wall above. Higher Nabbs farm drive is joined, go left on it to the road then right to reach Greenway Bridge.**

Without crossing the bridge take a stile on the right and head upstream in the company of a chirpy little brook. On reaching a slab bridge, cross and advance a little further with the wall before a green path branches left with the tiny Oaken Clough. Reaching a ruinous stone hut, there is a brief choice of ways. The public path continues up the stream side before rising to a stile and up towards the big house at Oakenclough.

However, a concession path avoids the house on a better line, distinctively bridging the brook and rising up the other side. It runs on to a stile then on through new plantings and by a pond to join the drive. Go right a few yards then take a stile on the left. A good path climbs away to a stile onto High Moor. Pause to look back over the two houses to a new perspective on Shutlingsloe (now revealing a pudding-like top).

A grand path heads away, running past a reedy pond to a wall corner. If a sign is still here advising of the option of a concession path across High Moor back to the forest start, then my experience suggests ignoring it: on my visit it was nothing less than a bulldozed quagmire. I wouldn't be paid to walk it, never mind recommend it, which makes it all the more galling to think that someone else is being paid our money for it to even exist! To be fair, it is intended to be improved, and possibly already is. **Keep on to the far corner of the moor. From the gateway the path goes right to a stile, then descends as an enclosed way (Macclesfield is in view down on the plain) to emerge onto a road, conveniently sited alongside the *Hanging Gate* pub.** The sign bears a short verse.

> This gate hangs here
> and troubles none
> refresh and pay
> and travel on

Turn right along this back road for a long mile's finish, which becomes even quieter as we keep straight on when it drops down to the left. Simply remain on this road to finish, keeping right at subsequent junctions. The views are superb, looking across the valley to Tegg's Nose (and of course the forest). An odd little building at whitewashed Higher Hardings Farm bears a lintel dated 1692.

Descending to a bend to enter the forest, an optional finish through the trees branches right just after the bend. As a track climbs away, a path sets off to run parallel with the road. On reaching a forest road, cross over and on a clear path opposite (signed to Shutlingsloe, but don't panic). This rises briefly then runs on to meet the outward track. The start is just five minutes down to the left. Before leaving cross the road to a little path in the trees to savour the pleasant water's edge scene on Trentabank Reservoir.

On Shutlingsloe, looking to the Roaches

14

MACCLESFIELD FOREST

START Tegg's Nose Country Park   Grid ref. SJ 950732

DISTANCE 6 miles

ORDNANCE SURVEY MAPS
1:50,000
Landranger 118 - Stoke-on-Trent & Macclesfield
1:25,000
Outdoor Leisure 24 - Peak District, White Peak

ACCESS Start from Tegg's Nose Country Park visitor centre off the A537 east of Macclesfield. Served by Buxton-Macclesfield buses on Saturday and Summer Sunday/BH Monday.

Don't let the modest distance disguise the 'up and down' work involved. A grand ramble however, delving deep into the forest without ever becoming claustrophobic, with attractive reservoirs, good woodland paths, fine views and some history too.

S Tegg's Nose Country Park is run by Cheshire County Council, and the visitor centre includes information, shop, refreshments and toilets. **From the visitor centre return to the road and go left on the parallel footway.** Almost at once an old milestone records *2 miles to Maccleffield* (sic), *163 miles to London*, an indication of the road's former importance.

The path quickly breaks off the road and rises to enter the heathery knolls of the country park proper. A few steps rise left then the path runs broadly past a long reclaimed quarry hole and onto the 'edge'. Keep straight on the left-hand way to reach an open air museum beneath curious quarried cliffs. Quarrying ceased here in 1955, and several former quarrying implements are laid out, along with a good little exhibition on millstone grit and its many uses.

Forging on, a vast quarry bowl is passed and super views are earned out over the valley to the forest, featuring the graceful cone of Shutlingsloe rising proudly above the dark tree line. Keep left above the rim. Rounding a corner above Tegg's Nose at the end, the path runs along to a stile as it appears to double back. From the stile a well-graded path enjoys a prolonged descent along the edge of the park in colourful open terrain. A wall comes in on the right as we drop into trees and down wooden steps to a small car park.

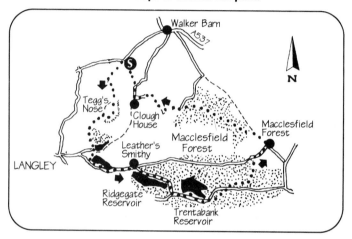

Head out of the country park over the dams of two small reservoirs (Teggsnose and Bottoms), divided by a narrow lane. Curve round the far side of the latter to join the road there. The robust profile of Tegg's Nose is now best seen rising beyond the water and the trees. A mile or so of road walking begins here, with the benefits of directness, a good pub, and splendid views over Ridgegate Reservoir. **Head along the road past the reservoir head, rising, partly with a footway to the *Leather's Smithy* pub.** This splendid hostelry enjoys a delightful location on the edge of both Ridgegate Reservoir and the forest itself.

Head along the reservoir-side road to a junction just past the forest office. A footway runs the short way to North West Water's Trentabank visitor centre. Though very different in character, the modern Macclesfield Forest revives the name of an ancient hunting forest, and indeed red deer can sometimes be spotted here. The visitor centre has a car park, picnic site and forest trails.

From the visitor centre a parallel path runs east with the road, quickly joining it again as a forest road turns off. **Keep straight on the road, passing the shore of Trentabank Reservoir.** This eastern end boasts the largest heronry in the National Park, and is leased to Cheshire Wildlife Trust. **Beyond the reservoir head a footway helps us along, rising round a bend to find a stile on the right. Here a concession path heads off into the trees.** It claims to cut the bending road but in fact runs parallel with it!

Rejoining the road cross straight over to a continuing path, this time straying further from the road. This broad path rises then runs on to a T-junction with a public footpath by a small pool. Go left on this path which climbs steeply (ignore a branch right to Standing Stone) out of the forest. It rises alongside some native trees, a good pull up onto a back road. Look back for a summit glimpse of Shutlingsloe.

Go right for a couple of minutes under colourful Toot Hill to reach the hamlet of Macclesfield Forest. In front, at more than 1300ft above sea level, is the church of St. Stephen, known as Forest Chapel. Above the porch a 1673 datestone from the original chapel is complemented by one recording its rebuilding in 1834. The church is renowned for

St. Stephen's, Forest Chapel

its August rushbearing service, more frequently witnessed in several Cumbrian villages. The tradition dates back to the times of earthen floors, when each year the old 'carpet' of rushes would be replaced by freshly cut ones. Today the ceremony extends to local rushes being interwoven with flowers to decorate the church, witnessed by an unnaturally large congregation. Across the road is the old school-house.

At this junction turn sharp left before the church, up a rough walled lane which climbs to the forest edge. This is part of the ancient Macclesfield Forest Ridgeway, used down the centuries and for long an important packhorse route. If staying on it, it will lead all the way over the tops to Walker Barn, from where it is only half a mile back to the start. **Our way takes a stile into the forest and an excellent path heads off into the trees.** This is super, a firm path, native trees lining much of the way, and breaks for views.

The path descends more steeply further on, through a newly planted area to the landmark of Dimples barn on a forest road. This is also a crossroads of footpaths. Ours crosses straight over, along the front of the derelict barn. At an early fork bear left, running on to leave the forest by a stile onto a narrow lane. Turn down here to its surfaced demise at Hardingland. Now we can enjoy good views across to the steep, colourful slopes of Tegg's Nose again, and identify our final stage, the Saddlers Way climbing back to the start.

To London 68 miles

Go left on the ensuing contrastingly unmade narrow section of lane (Forest Road) but almost at once a stile offers a short-cut down the field to rejoin the lane. Continue down, rough and stony for a while before easing out prior to another drop down to Clough House Farm. Go right a short way on the road out, then deflect left up the setted path of the Saddlers Way. The painstaking restoration of this historic packway was completed in 1987. **This rises unfailingly and relatively easily to emerge at the top plum on the start of the walk.**

Milestone, Old Buxton Road

15

DOVE HEAD

START Axe Edge   Grid ref. SK 034697

DISTANCE 7¾ miles

ORDNANCE SURVEY MAPS
1:50,000
Landranger 119 - Buxton, Matlock & Dove Dale
1:25,000
Outdoor Leisure 24 - Peak District, White Peak

ACCESS Start from Cistern's Clough car park on a sidelined loop of the A53, 3 miles south of Buxton. Served by Leek-Buxton express bus (Hanley-Sheffield) and Summer weekend/BH Monday Buxton-Roaches buses.

A fascinating exploration of the very upper reaches of the celebrated river Dove, far from the madding crowds that tramp its better known banks downstream.

❺ Axe Edge is a wild tract of moorland well known to motorists on the Buxton-Leek road high across its flank, one of several climbing out of Buxton that suffer the consequences of hard winters. The highest point of the moor is at 1807ft/551m, to the north of the starting point. Axe Edge's proudest claim to fame is as the source of no less than five notable rivers: the Dove, Manifold, Dane, Goyt and Wye are all born within close compass high on its flanks.

Leave the rear of the car park by a broad path rising above the upper reaches of Cistern's Clough. At once there is a sweeping view east, with Chrome Hill stunning amongst several lesser limestone peaks. **The path curves up to join a moorland road, head along to the brow.** Revealed on the skyline ahead is the *Cat & Fiddle*, England's second highest pub, with the elegant profile of Shutlingsloe further left.

Ignore the first track left on the brow and advance a further 100 yards; as the road starts a gentle descent take a grassy track off to the left. This runs across the moor past a peaty streamlet at the very headwaters of the Dane. Directly ahead, four miles distant, is the domed crest of the Roaches. **Striding south, when the main path bears right towards the wall ahead take a thin branch left. This crosses the head of a suddenly forming clough and slants gently up the slope before running along to the prominent Five Stones.** On their little knoll, these gritstone boulders are distinctive landmarks. **Here is another fork. Our way goes left (just before the stones), curving down through heathery tussocks to join a drive.**

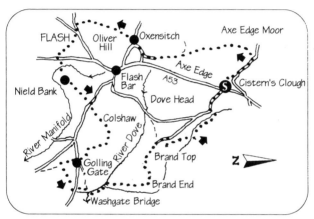

Go left on the drive, enjoying views over these colourful western moorlands. When it swings left go ahead to the gate in front, and a green, part-walled track runs on and down onto a lanehead by a house. Go straight down to a T-junction. Immediately in front is heather-covered Oliver Hill, at 1683ft/513m the highest point in Staffordshire, overtopping the Roaches by 26ft/8m.

Turn right to another T-junction at Oxensitch Farm. Go right a few yards then take a stile on the left, past the buildings and rising to a pair of stiles onto open moor. A good path rises away, passing through further stiles and onto the brow of the hill, and a low ruin. Heathery slopes on the left rise quickly to the crest of Oliver Hill, while ahead is an absorbing picture of the Back Forest/river Dane scene. **Advance on, slowly dropping down and absorbing a walled way**

from the right. The path broadens and soon becomes enclosed itself. At a fork leave the grassy lane through a gate/stile on the left, and a pleasant path runs through a couple of fields, dropping down to the side of a cottage where it rejoins the lane. Go left along the front of the cottages down onto a road. Go left into Flash.

Flash lays claim to being Britain's highest village, and at 1518ft/463m it also boasts the highest parish church. Though Flash is its undisputed focal point, the actual parish name is Quarnford. St. Paul's church was rebuilt in 1901, its squat tower barely higher than the nave roof. We also pass the impressive stepped front of a Wesleyan Methodist Chapel of 1784, rebuilt in 1821. The *New Inn* is the country's highest village pub, and the third highest of any pub in the land.

At the junction by the church a drive turns down the side of the churchyard, then go left along the rear of the farm buildings into a farmyard. Cross to a stile/gate opposite and head away on a track. At the end keep straight on to a stile in front, and maintain this wall-side line through stiles back onto the A53. Go straight over to a gate, and the left-hand of two footpaths. The scene in front is a grand one, presenting the opening half-mile of the river Manifold winding through a deep clough. **The bulldozed track leads us across the stream and along to the renovated house at Nield Bank.**

At the house the path forks. Bear left up a slanting way, quickly rising more steeply but pleasantly up the colourful broomy bank. Soon easing, it bears right along the top of the steep bank. The ensuing half-mile enjoys glorious views down over the already deep valley of the infant Manifold. **At the end a stile appears in a fence corner ahead. From it bear gently right down the field to another stile, then follow the wall away (past a little stone hut) to a stile onto a road junction.**

Go straight across on the cul-de-sac road. Grand views remain, now with the upper Dove scene taking over. **Keep on to its demise, becoming a rough track into a field (left). Don't take it, but take a stile on the right. An old part-hollowed way descends the fieldside, winding down to a bridle-gate alongside a tiny stream.** Here we are treading the course of one of countless packhorse routes that threaded a tortuous way through the hills of the Staffordshire moorlands: more are to follow. **Go left, quickly forking right to another such gate to cross the stream. An improved green walled way heads away, rising onto another narrow back road at Hillend.**

Go right a few yards then take the rough lane along the rear of the farm opposite at Golling Gate. This improves into a walled green way rising to the house at Moseley, with a 1775 datestone. Don't join the drive but take a stile in the low wall and descend the field. Ahead, Chrome Hill peeps over attractive hills but soon vanishes. **The field tapers between wall and stream to a stile onto a narrow road. Go left a few yards and from a stile head upstream above a small brook. A faint path runs at mid height, through a crumbling wall and on to a stile onto a rough lane. This drops down to turn a corner to suddenly confront the prospect of Washgate Bridge on the river Dove.**

Washgate Bridge is a real gem, hidden from the outside world in a timewarp from packhorse days. Now only visited by discerning walkers, centuries ago this was a meeting place for a staggering number of old ways. A study of the OS map reveals no less than eight paths and tracks converging on this gloriously colourful corner. Unlike so many other former packhorse bridges, still nothing more than a pack pony could negotiate this one. Don't be in a hurry to leave!

Washgate Bridge

Across, take the stony, spiralling way, enjoying a steep cobbled section. Look out for a stile on the left at one of these hairpin bends, from it a path runs upstream though grand country. This is an autumnal Arcadia as we traverse the bank of scrub, birch and bracken with the lively stream below. Ahead is a glimpse of the alarmingly high looking Axe Edge. **At the end the path drops to a confluence of twin streams: that on the left is the Dove.** The other, however, which we shall trace, makes a strong case for being the true source, being greater in length and starting at higher altitude.

Cross the stone slab bridge to a stile behind, from where a path climbs the steep nab. At the top bear right above the bracken bank, running along the crest of this steep drop to the stream below. After an intervening wall-stile a wall joins for company along to an isolated cottage. At a gateway beyond, a fine prospect of this upland hideaway opens out, with Thirkelow Rocks among the limestone hills across it. **A green track descends to the shell of Brand End Farm. Bear left of the ruin to the rising wall, and climb with it as far as a stile at a bend. Cross and resume up the other side to a gate. Through it a track rises to something of an eyesore at Shop Farm. Follow its drive out, and on through the fields past a dewpond to Brand Top Farm.**

Keep straight on up the improving road at Brand Top, passing a war memorial and former school. The little memorial garden recalls numerous members of the local community who fell in the Great War, 5 of the 12 victims sharing the same surname. **At the first opportunity, opposite a house on the left, take a gate on the right (the second of two) and a drive slants down the open field. Entering a small plantation it runs on to Birds Farm.**

Pass to the right of the outhouse to a gate/stile into a field where two paths head away. Slant right, through an old gateway and down a faint way past a barn to a footbridge on Cistern's Clough with the house at Fairthorn behind. Rise up the garden side, then turn left along the front of the house, soon emerging into open country. A delectable green track heads away, contouring round the slopes in this 'hidden' deep-cut valley. Directly ahead is Axe Edge, while below we pass a charming waterfall. **The way runs on to a bridge, crossing the stream and rising onto the narrow road serving Brand Top and Dove Head. Turn right, a few minutes' traffic-free pull to the main road, with the car park conveniently straight across.** In the final stages Chrome Hill returns to the scene, a nice flourish.

16

GOYT'S MOSS & GRIN LOW

START *Buxton*   *Grid ref. SK 048720*

DISTANCE *8¼ miles*

ORDNANCE SURVEY MAPS
1:50,000
Landranger 119 - Buxton, Matlock & Dove Dale
1:25,000
Outdoor Leisure 24 - Peak District, White Peak

ACCESS *Start from Grin Low car park on Grin Low Road, off the A53 Leek road. Alternative starts are Poole's Cavern on Green Lane, south of the town centre (GR 050725), or Goytsclough Quarry car park, half-way round in the upper Goyt Valley (GR 011734). Buxton is served by bus from surrounding towns, and by rail from Manchester.*

A splendid leg-stretcher from the fringe of Buxton to the rolling moors around the upper reaches of the Goyt Valley.

S Buxton is the true capital of the Peak District, even though the National Park boundary draws a discreet line around the town and its girdle of quarries. Roads radiate in all directions, both out of the Peak and into the heart of it. Many are of Roman origin, for the invaders settled in *Aquae Arnemetiae* due to the presence of the spring water. These waters rose to prominence in the 18th century, when the 5th Duke of Devonshire set out to create a spa town to rival Bath.

The Duke had the Crescent designed in the 1780s by the celebrated architect John Carr of York, and further buildings of note include the Opera House and the Pavilion. Visitors are also drawn to the Pump Room (now the Micrarium) with St. Ann's Well freely dispensing spa water alongside. Buxton Museum and the Pavilion Gardens are among countless other features that merit an extended amble round the streets, with the bustling Market Place presenting an animated scene.

The start is based in the vast hole of the former Grin Quarry. After thirty years being worked for limestone, it has seen imaginative restoration by the county council. The quarry floor is now home to a caravan site adjacent to the public car park and toilets. It was opened in 1989 and tree planting during the landscaping process is already bearing fruit.

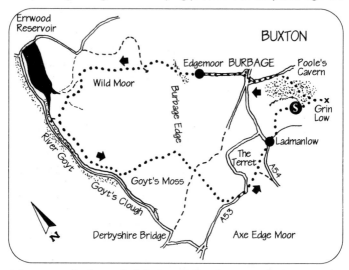

Advance to the far end of the car park, where a path rises past the edge of the quarry to immediately escape onto a corner of the open country of Grin Low. Solomon's Temple is directly ahead now. Advance on the wallside path outside the wood, reaching a stile and footpath sign just in front of a pond. We shall return to this point after the short detour to the folly, the obvious way leading to it.

Grin Low is the site of a Bronze Age burial chamber. The folly was erected in 1896 by Solomon Mycock as a source of employment, and was restored in 1987. Already at an altitude of 1440ft/439m, internal steps can be climbed to add that little extra to the sweeping panorama. Needless to say much of the Peak is outspread, with Buxton, several hundred feet below, backed by the sombre Kinder Scout skyline.

Return to the stile and into Grinlow Woods, where a broad path descends through the trees to a path crossroads above Poole's Cavern, with steps down to the car park. The natural cave of Poole's Cavern has been a showcave since Victorian times. Intermittently used since the Stone Age, it acquired its present name after sheltering a 15th century outlaw. A spacious interior boasts impressive limestone formations, with the infant river Wye also in attendance. The visitor centre has an exhibition, gift shop, toilets and picnic site. The cave is normally open from Easter to October.

From the car park entrance turn left along Green Lane. Swing right at the end in front of the Post office/shop and down to the *Duke of York* pub. Go down to its right onto the main road. To the left is Burbage parish church, Christ Church. **Cross straight over and down Nursery Lane. This quickly leaves the houses behind and runs on as Bishop's Lane to Plex Lodge.**

Keep straight on the private looking road, passing various buildings and rising away. Before the next house take a stile into loose woodland on the left. A path climbs steeply away, easing out to slant right towards the top corner of Beet Wood. A ladder-stile admits onto rolling grassy moorland. The path bears away to the right, very quickly gaining the brow above the Goyt Valley. Ahead, the Shining Tor/Cats Tor ridge appears across the gulf of the valley, while to the right is lonely Combs Moss. **The path drops to a crumbling wall corner then turns left down the wall-side, quickly arriving at a former railway line.** Just to the left is the blocked tunnel entrance.

The Cromford & High Peak Railway was completed in 1831 to link the Peak Forest Canal at Whaley Bridge with the Cromford Canal south of Matlock. Though the central section at Parsley Hay high on the limestone plateau survived into the 1960s, this western part closed in the late 19th century. Upon final closure in 1967, Derbyshire County Council and the Peak National Park took up the challenge of converting the 17½ miles from just beyond Buxton to Cromford into the High Peak Trail for walkers, cyclists and equestrians. For more on the Goyt Valley section see WALK 19.

Crossing straight over, the path resumes through a couple of crumbling walls and down the slope to ease out at Wildmoorstone Brook. Over to the left are the heathery slopes of Wild Moor. **Crossing the stream the path now runs a pleasant course well above it, circling**

round to a path junction before dropping to join a broad track. Turn left on this over the stream and curve round this side valley. Errwood Reservoir soon makes its appearance backed by the plantation slopes of Foxlow Edge. The reservoir was completed as recently as 1967 to provide water for Stockport. With a capacity of 927 million gallons it complements the unseen Fernilee Reservoir immediately down-dale.

After swinging left round a bend the ways fork. As the track climbs away, take the thinner path remaining with the wall. This runs on, passing through it and enjoying super views over the full extent of the reservoir and across to the wooded slopes of Shining Tor and Cats Tor. Turning away from the reservoir, the path runs through gloriously colourful terrain updale with the infant Goyt. After Goytsclough Quarry car park appears opposite, the path forks. Though our way is straight on, a brief diversion down to the right brings us to Goyt's Bridge. This charming packhorse bridge had to be removed here as a result of the reservoir construction. Goytsclough Quarry was where the Pickfords removal firm started out - with packhorse trains!

Goyt's Bridge

Back on the upper path, resume upstream in grand fashion, contouring round to reach a wooden footbridge. Again don't cross, but continue on a few yards to find the path departing the main valley in favour of Berry Clough. Here begins the climb back out, a

pleasant, sustained easy rise over Goyt's Moss. After crossing the stream a final steeper pull leads to a cairn marking a fork. Go right, the path running along the watershed to arrive at a rough road.

This is farewell to the Goyt Valley as we join the old Macclesfield-Buxton turnpike road of the mid-18th century. A hundred yards down to the right is an old milestone, the *Maccleffield* (sic) side still decipherable. The views are now of wide rolling moorscapes, with Axe Edge straight ahead. Over to the left behind the former Grin Quarry, Solomon's Temple can be discerned on Grin Low, with the tree-crowned Terret to the right.

Our way goes briefly left before taking a stile on the right. A splendid old green mine path heads away, passing a shaft and a small pool. Keep left at the end to a stile just short of the A54. Advance a few yards and go left on a thin trod before joining the road. Head down the verge for two minutes to a bend, then keep straight on the rough road in front. Just over the brow it drops down to the right: here keep straight on a broad, faint grassy way slanting beneath the windswept tree-topped Terret.

Pass through a gate in the wall below and down a fence-side with a covered reservoir on the right. At the corner, slant down to a small iron gate onto the Leek road. Cross to the junction at Ladmanlow and turn right along Grin Low Road. After a couple of minutes go left on the drive back into the car park.

Solomon's Temple, Grin Low

17

GOYT & DANE HEADS

START *Goyt's Moss*   *Grid ref. SK 018715*

DISTANCE *8¾ miles*

ORDNANCE SURVEY MAPS
1:50,000
Landranger 118 - Stoke-on-Trent & Macclesfield
Landranger 119 - Buxton, Matlock & Dove Dale
1:25,000
Outdoor Leisure 24 - Peak District, White Peak

ACCESS *Start from Goyt's Moss car park above Derbyshire Bridge, just off the A537 east of the Cat & Fiddle. The main road is served by Buxton-Macclesfield buses on Saturdays and Summer Sundays/BH Mondays.*

A high level, generally easy moorland stride on good paths, dipping into the heads of two famous Peakland rivers (each with their own fine clough scenery) but never dropping into the true valleys - the walk's lowest point is 1150ft/350m at Three Shires Head.

S The car park sits astride the junction of the Goyt Valley road with the former Buxton-Macclesfield turnpike, replaced by the higher level modern road in 1823. **Leave the car park by a green path rising away from the top end. The path narrows as it crosses a minor clough, going up it with an old wall to join a clearer path. Go right on this to rise to a broad track at a junction of crumbled walls.** This is the original Buxton-Macclesfield road, replaced by the turnpike in 1759.

Turn left along it to rise gently to a brow, with the A537 parallel to the right. Looking back we have the *Cat & Fiddle* on the skyline and Shining Tor's broad back to its right; further right, northwards, is the Goyt Valley. Alongside the track are the grass covered mounds of old mine workings, while ahead, parts of Buxton are revealed. **Briefly descend the other side just as far as a stile. Don't cross it, but just beyond it a thin trod runs across rough ground to join the adjacent road. Cross straight over to a gate from where an inviting footpath runs across the moor.**

A hollowed way soon branches left to join a broad former mine track alongside an old shaft, though our own path continues a little further before swinging left to join the broad green track. Bear right along this for a grand march across the moor to join a quiet road. The views are of uncompromisingly wide moorscapes, wonderful and bleak.

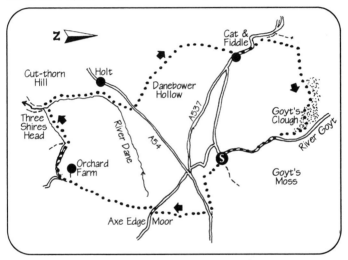

Go right fifty yards then resume along another distinct grassy way. Crossing an early trickle, pause to witness the first tentative moments of the river Dane. **The path runs across Axe Edge Moor to an acute wall corner, with a stile in the wall just down to the right.** Pause again to appraise Shutlingsloe's tilted, Ingleborough-like profile to the west. Axe Edge is over to the left, while ahead is a brief peek at the more distant Roaches' rocky crest. **The path resumes down the pasture, swinging left to join another firm green track. Go right down this, parallel with the lively clough. At the bottom it meets the Orchard Farm road. Go left down this to meet a back road on another such bend.**

Turn down to the right and in the company of the tiny beck follow this traffic-free farm road to the bottom. When it climbs to Blackclough Farm, stay with the stream on the rough track ahead. This remains our course, dropping down past one bridge and through a deep sided clough before arriving at the celebrated beauty spot at Three Shires Head. Here the counties of Derbyshire, Cheshire and Staffordshire meet, and our erstwhile stream swells the youthful Dane. Principal feature is the shapely arched bridge astride a delectable waterfall into Pannier's Pool (an apt name at this meeting place of old packhorse ways), a scene replicated on a smaller scale on the sidestream.

Resume by turning right, a broad path accompanying the Dane up through another deep, colourful clough. At a gate the green track rises up the pasture, but our footpath takes a stile on the right. This ensures close company with the stream on a sometimes faint path. Swinging round the corner with the busy A54 high above, we arrive at ruinous mine buildings. A sharp contrast awaits as the way becomes a broad green mine track slanting up towards a prominent tower above. The old green road doubles back left but advance through the stile in front for a steep pull beneath the tower onto a contrastingly green track. The tower is an air shaft from the old mine workings. Directly across the clough are the extensive scars of large scale workings, with tumbles of spoil fanning down into the stream.

Unfortunately the green track does not serve our needs, so cross the stile and turn up the slope again to emerge onto the A54. Straight across, a broad bridlepath rises into Danebower Hollow. We are accompanied by an intermittent deep boundary ditch, and this same track leads unfailingly over the broad moor. A guidepost sends a branch path down Cumberland Brook to Wildboarclough. **Swinging round, first Shining Tor is eventually revealed, then the mirage that is the *Cat & Fiddle*. The track now makes a bee-line for the pub: don't get knocked down rushing over the busy road in desperation!**

The *Cat & Fiddle* is the second highest pub in England, topped only by the *Tan Hill Inn* on the moors above Swaledale high up the Pennines. A challenge of walking the 120 miles to link the two originated in 1952 to mark the 50th anniversary of the Rucksack Club, hoping, presumably, to coincide with licensing hours on reaching the other end! A quick, easy finish to our more modest excursion (for those who over imbibed?) is to go right along the road to quickly branch off on the back road leading directly down to the start point.

Those made of sterner stuff will strike north along the road verge for a couple of minutes before branching right at a bend onto the firm base of the old turnpike road. It still has some of its original surface in place: note an old milestone *'to Maccleffield* (sic) *6 miles, to London 164 miles'*. A branch drops left down to the road but our way rises right, running a grand course along the moor to a tapering wall junction. From a stile on the right a clear path descends steeply with an old wall. Across the moor the location of the start point can be discerned. At the bottom we approach the head of a plantation.

Beyond the tiny stream of Stake Clough a track climbs out of the trees. Cross straight over and remain hard by the tree-line, soon reaching a stile into the woods. A good path heads away, dropping to a stream crossing in a clearing at Deep Clough. Up the other side, pass a ruined farm and along a level green way to the edge of the wood. With the splendour of Goyt's Clough revealed, a green path is joined. Turn right on it, narrowing as it runs on through bracken to emerge onto the road climbing through Goyt's Clough. Turn right to finish, crossing the quaintly curved Derbyshire Bridge to quickly reach the starting point.

Three Shires Head

18

SHINING TOR

START *Goyt Valley*   *Grid ref. SK 012748*

DISTANCE *6½ miles*

ORDNANCE SURVEY MAPS
1:50,000
Landranger 118 - Stoke-on-Trent & Macclesfield
Landranger 119 - Buxton, Matlock & Dove Dale
1:25,000
Outdoor Leisure 24 - Peak District, White Peak

ACCESS *Start from the Forestry Commission's Errwood Hall car park alongside Errwood Reservoir. On Sundays/BH Mondays (May-September) the road between the Street and Derbyshire Bridge is closed to avoid congestion and restore a little sanity to this popular spot. At all other times it is one way (southbound only). An alternative start is the Forestry Commission's Pym Chair car park on the route (SJ 994766).*

A smashing walk through the varied landscape of the Goyt Valley to the highest hill in the area. The first section is on concession paths.

S The Goyt Valley - properly Dale o'Goyt - is a major scenic attraction, a deep, colourful valley twice exploited in the desire to store water for nearby Stockport's growing urban populations. The pioneering traffic-free scheme for the valley was revolutionary when first used in 1970. Even then, traffic congestion on the dale's tiny, long-suffering road was entirely destroying the very thing people were seeking. **Leave the car park by a path climbing the open pasture behind. Bear right to the narrow gap in the wall to enter the trees. Just through, a broad path is joined. Turn right along this, following then crossing the stream before rising to a hairpin bend and junction. Swing right here to arrive at the ruins of Errwood Hall.**

Errwood Hall was home to a locally important Roman Catholic family, having been built in 1830 by Samuel Grimshawe as a wedding present for his son. The last member (Samuel's grand-daughter) died in 1930 after which Stockport Corporation moved in with a keen eye on the dale's water storage capabilities. The scant remains appear today as a folly-like ruin, featuring a shield set into the front doorway.

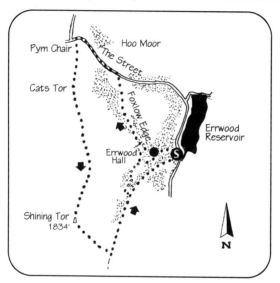

Leave by going left of the hall (woodland walk) where a broad path heads back into the trees. This runs on to merge at forlorn gateposts into the earlier track, advancing just a little further to more ruins on the edge of open country, remains of estate workers' cottages. A short detour from here leads to the Grimshawes' burial ground: simply turn up a thin path on the near side of the ruins, which quickly broadens and climbs the wooded knoll to find the site on the very top.

Beyond the cottages a path runs across our broad track. Here turn right down the pasture to a flight of steps to a footbridge on a brook. Just across is another path crossroads. This time go left, a well worn path slanting up beneath the woods, through a gap between sparse woodlands. Advance straight on the improving path, slanting up before running more level above the trees under Foxlow Edge.

Just past a ruin at the top of the trees a short branch path leads to an intriguing circular building with a beehive roof, the Spanish Shrine. Dedicated to St. Joseph it was built by the Grimshawes in 1889 as a memorial to their one-time Spanish governess. The low door reveals a truly beautiful little altar, featuring a painted mosaic and numerous little statues and prayers. This is quite a moving place and one that should be treated with the utmost respect, of course.

Emerging a little humbled, steps climb back to the main path to run over open moorland to join a road known as the Street. This is a former Roman road but better known for more recent use as a salters' way, when trains of packhorses would carry loads of salt from the Cheshire Plain to markets further east. Look up to the ridge we shall very shortly be traversing; and see also hollow ways of historic pack routes at Oldgate Nick on the ridge. Turn uphill, in the happy company of a parallel path that leads all the way to the road summit at Pym Chair.

From a stile on the left commence the skyline walk to Shining Tor. The path is largely very good, the first section being particularly tastefully restored. There is an early glimpse of the shrine just above the treeline. With a wall for company the whole way, the path leads first over Cats Tor (with a few rocks over the wall) and down to a dip before the climb to Shining Tor's broad, level top. The return ridge is well seen to the left across Shooter's Clough. A ladder-stile accesses the Ordnance Survey column (S2773).

At 1834ft/559m this is the summit of the walk and the highest point on the Peak's western moors, overtopping Axe Edge by some 25ft/8m. A few rock outcrops just beyond the trig. point afford a splendid vantage and sandwich point. Finest feature of the view is the peak of Shutlingsloe to the south-west, a graceful cone that outshines Shining Tor by a fair margin. Also note the massive white dish at Jodrell Bank down on the Cheshire Plain. Much nearer, the location of the *Cat & Fiddle Inn* is confirmed by the mast alongside and the waggons labouring up towards it.

Bearing in mind there is no further access on this side of the wall, re-cross and resume on the made path dropping then rising to a gate/stile onto a splendid green way. The *Cat & Fiddle* is ten minutes along to the right for those inclined! This is England's second highest pub, and its door is passed in WALK 17.

Our way goes left, enjoying the track's welcome surface for an uncomplicated stride back down to the start. Simply remain on this the whole way, tasting spacious views over the Goyt Valley. Errwood Reservoir features strongly beyond the trees: as recently as 1967 it joined the earlier Fernilee Reservoir downstream to complete the transformation of the Goyt Valley. At a stile in the adjacent wall (optional return via Shooter's Clough*) our path slants down to a ladder-stile alongside a plantation, but remains in open country to drop down to cross a track and ultimately into the trees for the final minute back to the start.

*Optional return via Shooter's Clough: From the stile a good path slants down to the oakwood, doubling back beneath it then down again to cross the tiny stream. This is then followed downstream to quickly reach the ruined estate cottages, from where turn right and return on the broad track.

The Spanish Shrine

19

WINDGATHER ROCKS

START *Horwich End*   *Grid ref. SK 008798*

DISTANCE *7½ miles*

ORDNANCE SURVEY MAPS
1:50,000
Landranger 118 - Stoke-on-Trent & Macclesfield
Landranger 119 - Buxton, Matlock & Dove Dale
1:25,000
Outdoor Leisure 24 - Peak District, White Peak

ACCESS *Start from a car park on the A5004, on a sidelined bend of the road just south of Horwich End. Served by Whaley Bridge-Fernilee buses, while Horwich End and Whaley Bridge are more frequently served from Macclesfield, Buxton and Stockport. Rail station one mile away at Whaley Bridge.*

A varied walk in the Goyt Valley, from riverbank, reservoir shore and woodland to colourful moorland, sweeping views and the delights of the main objective.

❺ **Leave the car park by a bridle track descending steeply into the trees. Below is the river Goyt (and footbridge by which we shall return), but halfway down turn left at a stile on a bend. A broad path heads updale through the trees, ultimately ceasing at a stile out of the woods. A contrastingly faint path takes over for a smashing walk through the fields in the company of the sparkling Goyt.**

Passing a footbridge we merge into a waterworks track, through treatment works and rising as a service road to a junction. Go right to the edge of the grassy embankment of Fernilee Reservoir. After the dale was purchased by Stockport Corporation, Fernilee Reservoir was completed in 1938, and has a capacity of 1087 million gallons.

Next stage is to attain the dam of Errwood Reservoir, seen from the centre of the present dam. The easiest, quickest way remains on the east/left bank of Fernilee Reservoir. This follows the very direct course of the former Cromford & High Peak Railway, an ambitious project linking the Peak Forest Canal at Whaley Bridge with the Cromford Canal at Cromford, near Matlock. **Most interesting approach is to cross the dam and take a narrow road left into the trees. At the first bend go left over a stile into the woods. A clear path heads away, and at the first chance take a waymarked branch left nearer the shoreline, quickly dropping even closer.**

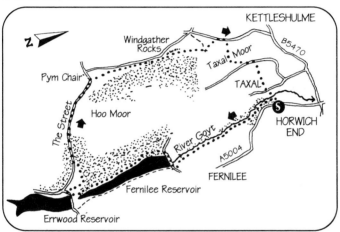

The path remains at shore level the full length of the reservoir. This is a fine amble as it marches near the waterline (depending on drought levels!), with wide breaks in the mixed woodland to look over the water. In not infrequent times of low water, several old walls can be seen running down into the dry head. Until completion of Errwood Reservoir a suspension footbridge crossed the upper reach of the reservoir on the line of the drowned section of Roman road known as the Street. **Towards the end (after a gate) a branch climbs away to the right: take either, for the main path also rises just beyond and they merge in open country just short of the road at the end of the dam.**

Errwood Reservoir was completed as recently as 1967, with a capacity of 927 million gallons. Its construction brought the demise of thousands of rhododendrons and attractively laid out walks between them, and also Goyt's Bridge, a charming packhorse bridge which had to be removed further upstream (see WALK 16). The reservoir supports a sailing club and offers good views beyond the water to the moors rising to Burbage Edge. A little further updale are the scant remains of Errwood Hall, once home of the influential Grimshawe family: this area is featured in WALK 18.

Directly across the water is the knoll of Bunsall Cob, above which can be seen the course of the former Bunsall Incline now overlaid by a road. This was one of nine inclines on the old railway, which became fully operational in 1831 with horse-drawn waggons linking the inclines. Within a dozen or so years, steam locomotives largely replaced the horses. For more than 20 years a passenger service also operated, though it took a full day to complete the journey: a fatal accident in 1877 brought that venture to a premature end. All the little stations were called wharves to complement the canal system: indeed, originally the entire route was optimistically mooted as a canal!

Here one could advance to the road junction ahead and turn right up the road known as the Street (a former Roman road leading to Buxton), but more interestingly without joining the road, double back on a broad grassy way to the right. This runs on to the ruins of the farm complex it once served, then on again to the edge of the plantation. Cross the fence-stile but don't enter the trees. Instead, turn left up the outside on a path climbing initially through dense bracken. This relents and the path swings round to join the Street at a forest road gate.

Turn uphill between plantations to enjoy a climb that doesn't involve setting foot on tarmac. A broad path climbs parallel to the road, all the way to its summit. Emerging from the trees there are views ahead to Cats Tor and the ridge to Shining Tor, high above the plantations. Easing out there are views left down the Foxlow valley, with dark plantations across it beneath the Cats Tor skyline leading to Shining Tor; then a short final pull affords the first sighting of Windgather Rocks over to the right. Currently however the greater view dominates, with the heathery edge of Hoo Moor leading the eye to the distant northern moors. Beyond Lantern Pike and Cracken Edge/Chinley Churn are Mount Famine and South Head beneath the long, high skyline of Kinder Scout.

Windgather Rocks, looking to Cats Tor

Just short of the road summit a stile on the right sends a path across the heather moor. The wide views are now swelled by distant features to the west, with flat, urban landscapes beyond the nearer rolling hills. **Reaching a stile onto the ridge road we needn't join this either, for a concession path keeps us on the moor side of the wall, leading very nicely indeed all the way along to Windgather Rocks. Here the road drops away, but a footpath rejoins our concession path to enjoy a smashing walk along the crest.** Windgather Rocks are a fine wall of gritstone outcrops, up to 30ft in height and tilted at a sufficiently accommodating angle to tempt scramblers amongst us into action: novice climbers are particularly well catered for here.

At the end of the main rocks cross a low wall and continue down the fieldside, now with a wall shielding the final minor outcrops of Taxal Edge. Drop to a stile in front of the farm ahead, and go left through a gate on the drive. Go immediately right over a stile and cross the small enclosure to a small gate left of the trees. From a stile just behind, slant down past a sheep bield (L-shaped shelter) to a stile, and down to another onto a narrow road. Kettleshulme sits in the valley below. **Go right, briefly, past a house to reach a stile by a gate, and head up the field to a ladder-stile onto the heather of Taxal Moor.**

Go straight ahead through the nick and a path descends through the heather. A grand view over the lower Goyt Valley and Whaley Bridge opens out. Alongside the path is an old hollowed way, now almost lost in the rampant heather. **The path swings left to run delightfully down through a mix of heather and rhododendrons to join the road. Go left for a minute or so to a ladder-stile on the right. This final stage crosses the fields in a direct descent punctuated by intervening stiles. At the bottom join a back road at Taxal and go left to the church.**

St. James' church (originally St. Leonard's) is a gem, sheltering in a leafy corner seemingly far from the outside world. The hoary tower dates back to the 16th century, the rest restored in 1889. Some fine old gravestones are set in the path outside, while a sundial affixed to a stone shaft is dated 1703. Just past the church is a private house that was until quite recently a pub known as *The Chimes*, dating back to the 17th century when it was the *Royal Oak*.

Conclude by turning down a steep, stony way on the near side of the church, passing between graveyards to debouch alongside the river Goyt at a ford. Go left to find the footbridge, with the car park just up the steep track above, on which we began.

LYME PARK

START Lyme Park   Grid ref. SJ 963822

DISTANCE 5¼ miles

ORDNANCE SURVEY MAPS
1:50,000
Landranger 109 - Manchester
1:25,000
Outdoor Leisure 1 - Peak District, Dark Peak

ACCESS Start from the car park in the grounds of the National Trust's Lyme Hall, accessed from the A6 at Disley. There is a substantial admission charge for cars: this is separate from the optional admission to the house itself (all free to NT members). Alternatives are to walk in (free) from Disley, served by bus (Buxton, Glossop, Stockport, Manchester) and Manchester-Buxton trains; or to park at the road top at Bowstonegate (on the route). If you're visiting the house and/or spending the day here, it's as easy to use the recommended start point to park. Sunday/BH Monday Glossop-Stockport buses also serve the main car park.

A leisurely ramble blending stately parkland with its attendant moorland. Includes a lengthy uphill section, but with ample rewards. To avoid confusion, remember the house itself is known as Lyme Park.

S Lyme Park dates from Elizabethan times, though only some mid-16th century sections remain within the major expansion of the 1720s. The magnificent Palladian-style south front is not unlike Chatsworth, indeed in many ways Lyme mirrors that grander house at the opposite side of the National Park. Surrounding the house are 16 acres of gardens, beyond which is a 1400 acre deer park: both red and fallow deer are likely to be seen during the walk. In 1995 Lyme Park was used as the exterior setting of Pemberley in the BBC adaptation of Jane Austen's *Pride and Prejudice*, a claim it is now able to play on to the full extent of its marketing powers. Lyme was home of the distinguished Legh family for six centuries until crippling running costs saw it handed to the National Trust in 1946.

Alongside the car park is an information and ice cream kiosk, while two minutes away by the lake are cafe, gift shop and toilets in restored estate buildings. Numerous special events take place throughout the season. All in all this is a delightful place to while away a summers' day. The park is open throughout the year, the house itself from Easter to late Summer, afternoons only, limited days.

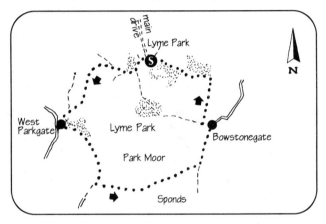

From the car park take the surfaced drive (not the main drive) south-west, left of the nearby lake. It curves away and rises to a brow. Keep right at a fork towards the wall on the right, but then fork left to run on beneath the minor knoll of Knott on our left. Ahead is a sweeping vista over the Cheshire Plain and Stockport's suburban sprawl. **The drive runs on to end in front of a stile/gate in a fence. A nicer track runs on, swinging left to run to a deer fence on the edge of the park.**

Through the kissing-gate the green track resumes in a large open pasture, dropping down to a stile/gate in the corner. Descend to a farm lane and go left down past West Parkgate to West Lodge. Don't re-enter the park here unless abandoning the walk, but head along the narrow lane to a junction outside a well maintained Methodist Chapel of 1861. Turn left up the adjacent drive, rising between

houses and by a wooded clough to a gate/stile into open pasture. **The path continues up the clough side, climbing outside the park wall.** To the left is the colourful clough of oddly named Cluse Hay, featuring a few rock outcrops. **Climbing above a stile the terrain opens out, and the lovely green path rises above a tiny side-stream before turning away from the isolated cottage at Moorside. Cross to a stile in the top corner, and go right along the drive beneath a stand of trees to reach Keepers Cottage.**

The guidepost here struggles with the long-winded names of Bowstonegate and Kettleshulme. **Resume the climb on a path up the side of the cottage. This rises pleasantly by an old wall to reach the brow on Dale Top at 1259ft/384m.** Revealed ahead now is a grand view including the Shining Tor/Cats Tor ridge with the peak of Shutlingsloe to the right. Kinder Scout also features beyond the white-walled Bowstones Farm, our next objective.

Pass through the fence-stile in front and bear left with the park wall. Over the wall is the extensive Park Moor, and within its bounds you are likely to spot a herd of red deer that roams here. **The path induces broad strides along the easy, undulating terrain of Sponds, around to join a firmer track.** The view east is now enhanced by a steeper drop to intervening valleys. **Go left on the track, quickly becoming enclosed to tread the broad, historic ridgeway along to the roadhead at Bowstonegate, with a cluster of masts behind Bowstones Farm.** In a little roadside enclosure are the Bow Stones, sections of two round shafted crosses of differing height, thought to be of Saxon origin.

Take a stile on the left and cross the field to a ladder-stile back into Lyme Park. The main path drops straight down the moor, but a nicer finish turns immediately right along the park wall. This path quickly reaches a brow marked by a memorial view indicator. At 1312ft/ 400m this also marks the summit of the walk. Beyond it as the house itself appears, path and wall drop down to a corner in front of a plantation. Ignoring the stile, our path runs left down the wallside, winding down to a stile/gate in the bottom corner.

Resume along a broader track past more trees to descend to the start, passing the north front of the hall. **The finest conclusion takes a gate on the left before reaching the house, to enter the fallow deer sanctuary. A path curves right, outside the south front of the house and the south lake to return to the car park over a tall ladder-stile.**

LOG OF THE WALKS

WALK	DATE	NOTES
1		
2		
3		
4		
5		
6		
7		
8		
9		
10		
11		
12		
13		
14		
15		
16		
17		
18		
19		
20		

INDEX

Principal features: walk number refers

THE PEAK DISTRICT

Explore on foot Britain's most popular National Park with a comprehensive set of 5 guidebooks. Each contains 20 walks.

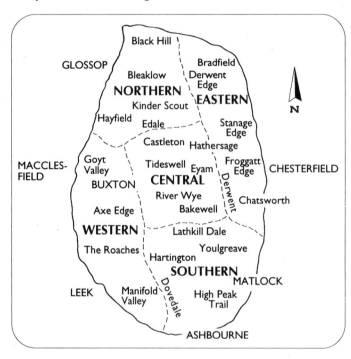

- **NORTHERN PEAK**   ISBN 1 870141 48 2
  Edale/Kinder Scout/Longdendale/Bleaklow/Hayfield/Mam Tor
- **EASTERN PEAK**   ISBN 1 870141 50 4
  Derwent Valley/Baslow/Eastern Edges/Chatsworth/Ladybower
- **CENTRAL PEAK**   ISBN 1 870141 51 2
  Bakewell/Wye Dale/Eyam/Monsal Dale/Tideswell/Miller's Dale
- **SOUTHERN PEAK**   ISBN 1 870141 52 0
  Dovedale/High Peak Trail/Lathkill Dale/Matlock/Tissington Trail
- **WESTERN PEAK**   ISBN 1 870141 54 7
  Buxton/The Roaches/Goyt Valley/Manifold Valley/Shutlingsloe